Essential Netherlands

by
POLLY PHILLIMORE

Polly Phillimore has made regular contributions to *Holiday Which?*
and other travel books published by the British Consumers'
Association. She has also written guides to the United Kingdom and
Morocco.

Produced by AA Publishing

Written by Polly Phillimore
Peace and Quiet section by
Paul Sterry
Series Adviser: Ingrid Morgan
Copy Editor: Christopher
Catling

Edited, designed and produced
by AA Publishing. Maps © The
Automobile Association 1993.

Distributed in the United
Kingdom by AA Publishing,
Fanum House, Basingstoke,
Hampshire, RG21 2EA.

The contents of this publication
are believed correct at the time
of printing. Nevertheless, the
publishers cannot accept
responsibility for errors or
omissions, nor for changes in
details given. Assessments of
attractions, hotels, restaurants
and so forth are based upon the
author's own experience and,
therefore, descriptions given in
this guide necessarily contain an
element of subjective opinion
which may not reflect the
Publisher's opinion or dictate a
reader's own experience on
another occasion.
**We have tried to ensure
accuracy in this guide, but
things do change and we
would be grateful if readers
would advise us of any
inaccuracies they may
encounter.**

A CIP catalogue record for this
book is available from the
British Library.

ISBN 0 7495 0516 8

Published by The Automobile
Association.

This book was produced using
QuarkXPress ™, Aldus
Freehand™ and Microsoft
Word™ on Apple Macintosh™
computers.

Colour separation by BTB
Colour Reproduction Ltd,
Whitchurch, Hampshire

Printed by: Printers Trento
S.R.L., Italy

*Front cover picture: Kinderdijk,
Zuid Holland province*

Contents

This book employs a simple rating system to help choose which places to visit:

 'top ten'

♦♦♦ do not miss
♦♦ see if you can
♦ worth seeing if you have time

Introduction and Background

INTRODUCTION

Although the Netherlands is a small country, it
has a remarkably varied landscape, and each
of the twelve provinces has its own distinctive
character.

The best known cities of the Netherlands are
located in the two provinces of Noord (North)
and Zuid (South) Holland. They include
Amsterdam, Den Haag (The Hague),
Rotterdam and a host of smaller towns, such as
Delft, Leiden (Leyden), Haarlem, Edam and
Gouda. All are renowned for their architecture,
the wealth of their many museums covering the
maritime history of the Netherlands, the long-
standing connections with Indonesia, and the
great works of art produced by Dutch masters
such as Rembrandt, Frans Hals and Vermeer.

The Regions

North and South Holland, together with the tiny province of Utrecht, form an area known to the Dutch as the *Randstad*, meaning 'ring town' – so called because its cities form one huge, almost circular, conurbation. The distances between the towns of the *Randstad* are so small that you can hop from one to the other in less than half an hour by train or car, and the people of the region refer to it affectionately as 'the big village'. It would be very easy to spend a rewarding week or fortnight in this area alone, enjoying the largely cosmopolitan pleasures of museums, night life and excellent, reasonably-priced restaurants. To do so, however, would be to miss the wilder and more traditional side of the Netherlands, the rural provinces where farmers and fishermen still fight an elemental battle with the land and sea to make a living and where the pace of life invites leisurely exploration on foot, by bicycle, by canoe or sailing dinghy.

Zeeland province, stretching south to the Belgian border, is a magical region where the landmass disintegrates into a jigsaw puzzle jumble of islands laced by inlets from the North Sea. Frequent flooding led to the construction of a massive complex of dams and storm barriers, known as the Delta Project and completed in 1986, which now protects this region from the worst excesses of the sea. These dams provide the islands with a superb road system; driving across the top of the barriers you can explore tiny fishing villages, famous for their seafood restaurants, discover empty beaches and a series of sheltered lakes that are a paradise for lovers of water sports. Nature lovers, too, will find much to see, especially in the southernmost part of the province, known as Zeeland Flanders, where the marshes and mud flats of the Scheldt estuary, designated as a nature reserve, attract a host of feeding birds.

Heading eastwards and inland, the two southern provinces of Noord Brabant and Limburg are different again. This is a hilly region, bordering on the foothills of the Belgian Ardennes, where the landscape is composed of gently wooded valleys and border castles

Well-preserved windmills dot the Dutch landscape

INTRODUCTION

The Kurhaus at Scheveningen, near Den Haag

perched on peaks high enough to justify the humorous epithet, the 'Dutch Alps'.

This region remained Catholic after the Dutch Revolt of the 16th century, when Calvinism became the predominant religion in the rest of the Netherlands, and this is reflected in the more flamboyant Gothic-inspired architecture of the region's churches and town halls. Carnival is a big event in the southern provinces and you will witness riotous celebrations if you visit in the weekend prior to Shrove Tuesday – Bergen in particular is noted for its traditional celebrations, when everyone, from children to pensioners, adopts a disguise and joins in festivities which date back to the time of Brueghel.

Heading north, the provinces of Gelderland and Overijsell are separated from the southern provinces by the great rivers of the Rijn (Rhine), Maas and Waal. Beyond lies a region of heath and woodland, much of it contained within the vast Hoge-Veluwe National Park, one of the Netherlands' most beautiful conservation areas. Art and nature complement each other at the centre of this park, where Europe's largest outdoor sculpture gallery surrounds the Kröller–Müller museum, housing over 250 works by the artist Vincent Van Gogh.

It is a short step from here to the peaceful green region known, aptly, as the *achterhoek*, the back corner, an area of the Netherlands that waits to be discovered by overseas visitors, but which the Dutch themselves already know and love for its meandering streams and flower-filled meadows, its orchards and marshlands where rare plants flourish. The landscape becomes increasingly wild further north, as you pass through the sparsely populated peat and moorland province of Drenthe, up to Groningen and Friesland. Here you will find the oldest inhabited parts of the Netherlands – the landscape is dotted with the remains of *hunebedden*, burial grounds built of great megalithic boulders around the 3rd and 4th centuries BC, and the region's museums contain intriguing wooden boats and artefacts discovered undecayed in the bogs. The houses are no longer built of peat, but there are numerous reed-thatched farmhouses perched on top of low mounds, or *terpen*, raised just high enough to keep dry in winter, and the streets really do echo to the sound of clattering clogs – worn for practical reasons, not for the sake of tourism.

The Dutch see this region as their historical homeland, the point from which they spread out to start the painstaking task of reclaiming new land from the sea. Friesians would reject this, being proud of the fact that they have their own language and a different ethnic heritage – the local tourist office even issues a special 'Friesland Passport' explaining the unique culture of this province, which jokingly talks about independence from the rest of the Netherlands. All comers are welcomed, however, and the region's lakes offer plenty of opportunity for camping, walking, canoeing and sailing. Another sport, practised only with an officially-registered guide, is *wadlopen* – mud walking – one way to cross the mud flats of the Waddenzee to reach the chain of tiny islands that stand between the Netherlands and the North Sea. Ferries provide a less strenuous means of access to these unspoiled islands, renowned for their bird life and long clean sandy beaches.

Red-roofed farmsteads on the island of Texel

Faced with such sheer variety, any visitor to the Netherlands can only hope to sample a small portion on a short holiday – enough, however, to whet the appetite for more; once visited, the Netherlands is a country to which travellers always vow to return.

BACKGROUND

The Netherlands is a tiny country by comparison with many of its European neighbours (about 120 miles (192km) east to west and 180 miles (288km) north to south), yet it has played a role in world history out of all proportion to its size; never before or since, wrote one historian, has such a 'complete and highly original civilisation sprung up in so short a time in so small a territory'.

In the 12th century, major cities, like Amsterdam, consisted of little more than a cluster of huts built by herring fishermen. From such humble origins, the Dutch rapidly developed a thriving trade with Germany, England and the Baltic ports, acting as a distribution point for cloth, grain, beer, timber, furs, salt and fish. By the end of the 13th century, many of the best-known cities of the Netherlands had already been granted municipal rights by their nominal rulers, the Counts of Holland and the Bishops of Utrecht, so that they were able to create and enforce their own laws. Trade was regulated by guilds, cities were ruled by burgomasters and a sheriff was responsible for law and order, assisted by militia volunteers. Membership of the militia was a matter of civic pride and open to anyone wealthy enough to afford the uniform and a pike or crossbow. Numerous portraits of militia members now fill the museums and art galleries of the Netherlands, including Rembrandt's famous painting in Amsterdam's Rijksmuseum, known as the *Night Watch*.

In addition to all this, quite a number of cities instituted planning laws which were very advanced for their time; after a series of disastrous fires, which destroyed whole town centres in the 15th century, building in timber and thatch was prohibited in favour of brick and tile. With this the characteristic appearance of so many ancient Dutch towns began to take shape.

The Dutch Revolt

At the beginning of the 16th century, the Netherlands had, as a result of war, treaties and marriage alliances, become part of the mighty Habsburg empire, ruled by the Spanish

NETHERLANDS

Holy Roman Emperor, Charles V. The country
was, thus, nominally Catholic, but many cities,
including Amsterdam, provided a haven for
Protestant minorities seeking refuge in Europe.
The Calvinists were a particularly large and
influential group, but they were forbidden from
holding public services. This caused
considerable tension which finally boiled over
in 1566; all through the Netherlands, Calvinists
rioted, sacking churches and monasteries, an
event that has gone down in Dutch history as
the *Beeldenstorm*, the Iconoclasm or 'image-
breaking'.

The Dutch responded in pragmatic fashion by allowing Calvinists their own churches in return for a restoration of order. This precipitated a swift response from Philip II of Spain, who had been crowned Holy Roman Emperor on the abdication of his father, Charles V. Philip saw himself as a staunch defender of the Catholic faith. In 1567 he sent an army into the Netherlands, led by the Iron Duke, Fernando Alvarez de Toledo. Ruthless methods were used to restore strict conformity with the Catholic religion – liberal city officials were replaced and many Protestants were publicly executed.

Dutch resentment against Spanish tyranny began to take a concrete form in 1572; the various city militias, whose role had previously been limited to that of maintaining law and order, now began to form into a volunteer army led by William the Silent, Prince of Orange. Starting in the north, Prince William's troops began to drive the Spanish from Dutch territory, city by city. It was a long, hard war, in which cities such as Leiden had to withstand long sieges, resulting in many deaths from disease and starvation. Amsterdam, one of the last cities to be liberated, finally fell to Prince William's troops in 1578, marking almost the end of the war. A peaceful revolution, known as the *Alteratie* (the Alteration) then occurred, as Protestants returned from exile to take over churches and city institutions. Calvinism became the state religion and from then onwards, until the 19th century, Catholicism was banned. Catholics did continue to worship, however, in hidden churches such as the attic church preserved in the roof of Amsterdam's Amstelkring Museum.

The following year, 1579, the seven northern provinces of the Netherlands effectively declared unilateral independence when they signed the Treaty of Utrecht. While each province retained independence, it allowed for joint action in the interests of mutual defence. The Spanish, meanwhile, entrenched themselves in Antwerp; many Protestants and Jews fled to Amsterdam, bringing with them the skills and resourcefulness that would help pave the way for the Golden Age.

William the Silent, Prince of Orange

The Golden Age

The newly independent northern provinces, full of self confidence, rapidly developed into a powerful trading nation. Ships set sail from Amsterdam in 1595 and 1598, intent on charting navigable routes to the spice islands of the East. Travelling via the Cape of Good Hope and the Indian Ocean, Dutch explorers penetrated further and further east, to Indonesia, China, Japan, Australia, Tasmania and New Zealand, coming back with ships laden with sugar, spices, tea and porcelain that sold for sky-high prices, making a handsome profit for the backers.

Soon hundreds of merchant ships were following in their wake, and Amsterdam experienced phenomenal growth as the trade in tropical products made the city prosperous. In 1602 the various businesses involved in Far East trade came together to form the Dutch East India Company. This established trading posts, which in time became virtual Dutch colonies. By 1669, at the peak of the Golden Age, the East India Company was the world's largest trading enterprise.

The West India Company, founded in 1621 to control trade with Africa and the Americas, was less successful; one of its trading colonies, New Amsterdam, was established by Peter Minuit in 1626 on the island of Manhatten; it is better known today as New York, renamed after the settlement was captured by the English in 1664.

As the Dutch empire expanded, so cities like Amsterdam needed more space for ships and warehouses. Wealthy merchants poured their money into the stately canalside houses that were built in many Dutch cities from the 1630s, and they furnished their homes with outstanding works of art. John Evelyn, Samuel Pepys and other visitors to 17th-century Amsterdam were amazed by the quantity of fine art on sale in the city. Amsterdam developed the first truly open market for art, which was sold through dealers, bookshops and auctioneers. Instead of art being the preserve of rich patrons and institutions, ordinary citizens could commission portraits of their houses, possessions, friends or even (as

The Calvinist uprising of 1566

BACKGROUND

in the case of Paulus Potter's *The Young Bull,* in the Mauritshuis Museum, Den Haag) of their prize animals.

Artists were assured of a constant supply of work, and the age gave birth to the towering talents of Frans Hals, Rembrandt, Jan Steen and Vermeer, not to mention a host of prolific lesser artists whose paintings now fill the country's museums.

The year 1689 perhaps marks the peak of the Netherlands' Golden Age; in that year, the Dutch prince, William III of Orange, was crowned King of England, Scotland, Wales and Ireland, as a result of his marriage to the English princess, Mary Stuart. England and the Netherlands, so often at war in the past, were now allies. In England, and further afield, everything Dutch – from gabled houses and water gardens to tulips, Delftware and landscape paintings – was fashionable. Amsterdam, too, was at the height of its powers, the biggest city of the Netherlands (population 220,000), the capital of an Empire stretching from Australia to the Antilles.

During the Golden Age, Dutch ships ruled the waves

The Modern State

During the 18th and 19th centuries the Dutch acted vigorously to defend their worldwide trading interests against competition. The result was a series of costly wars, principally with England and France, that slowly drained the Dutch economy and crippled its maritime trade. As swiftly as the nation had risen from nowhere, so it began to decline.

Even so, there were other vital forces at work. Jews began settling in large numbers, refugees from Spain, Portugal, Germany and Poland, enjoying freedoms in cities like Amsterdam and Rotterdam that were denied them elsewhere. They were prohibited from joining the powerful trade guilds, which effectively barred them from many areas of employment. Instead they introduced new processes, particularly diamond cutting and polishing, and the Jewish quarters of Dutch cities became a byword for enterprise and industry.

At the same time, the Netherlands was in a ferment of social unrest, frequently shaken by riots in protest against high levels of taxation, administrative corruption and undemocratic rule. In 1795 French revolutionary troops marched into the country to be welcomed by liberal reformers. A representative national assembly was created, but all constitutional reforms were reversed when Napoleon invaded Amsterdam in 1808 and declared his brother, Louis Napoleon, King of the Netherlands. Napoleon's intervention and the restoration of the old order after his defeat at Waterloo simply delayed the inevitable. Riots in Amsterdam in 1845 led to the appointment of J R Thorbecke as head of a constitutional commission whose recommendations led to the creation of a directly-elected parliament in 1849. Thorbecke himself led a series of governments that laid down the structure of the modern Dutch state, with its emphasis on welfare, education, housing and health care for all.

Dutch neutrality during World War II was ignored by the Nazis, who bombed Rotterdam in 1940 before invading the rest of the Netherlands. Many Dutch people reacted with heroism, striking in protest against anti-Jewish measures, and sheltering Jews, such as Anne Frank and her family, in cellars and secret back rooms.

Such acts of resistance were consistent with the long Dutch tradition of humanism, tolerance and liberalism. These ideals came increasingly to the fore in the post-war era, with the passing of permissive laws on homosexuality and the sale of cannabis and pornography. As a result, 'Swinging Amsterdam' became a hippy mecca in the 1960s and 70s. Violent clashes between police and demonstrators also became a regular feature of city life in the 1970s and early 80s, as young people staged sit-ins and squatted in empty houses, challenging every form of authority.

The protest movements of this period had the effect of concentrating official policy on urban renewal, and formerly run-down areas in many Dutch cities have since been transformed into lively communities. Further colour is added by the large numbers of Indonesian and Surinamese who have chosen to live in the Netherlands, migrants from former Dutch colonies who secured their independence shortly after the war.

Recent decades have also seen some major engineering achievements as this tiny, but densely populated country, has sought to find more and more land for its growing population and the needs of its important agricultural industry. In 1932 the monumental Afsluitdijk (Enclosing Dyke) was completed, damming the former Zuiderzee, now known as the IJsselmeer. Areas of this lake were then drained to create extensive areas of *polder*, the name given to newly reclaimed land. The first settlers moved into this new region in the 1960s, and as recently as 1986 the Flevoland polder was declared the 12th province of the Netherlands.

Such major projects reflect the continuing dynamism of the Dutch nation, a fascinating country which, after seven centuries, is still taking shape and in which the ultra-modern coexists alongside beautiful towns and villages where nothing much seems to have changed since the Golden Age.

What to See

The Essential rating system:

✓ 'top ten'

♦♦♦ do not miss
♦♦ see if you can
♦ worth seeing if
you have time

AMSTERDAM

Amsterdam is a delightful and welcoming city in which you will rapidly begin to feel at home. Amsterdam Centraal station forms the focal point of the downtown area; most visitors arrive here by train from Schiphol airport, and there are plenty of taxis waiting to take you on to your hotel. The **VVV tourist information centre** is opposite the magnificent station building, as is the office of the GVB transport authority where you can pick up maps of the metro, tram and bus system. Stationsplein, the busy square in front of the station, is the main tram terminus.

Also opposite the station are two waterways, called Rokin and Damrak, where several competing companies offer canal boat tours. Tours, lasting from one to three hours, depart at roughly half-hour intervals and are an ideal way of finding your feet; taped commentaries (in several languages) point out the city's major monuments as you cruise the canal system. If you

are arriving by car, you should ideally find a hotel with secure parking and forget the car for the duration of your stay, since driving and parking in the city centre are extremely difficult. Alternatively, you can park at Europarking, Marnixstraat 250, which is a short walk from the centre of Amsterdam.

Orientation

The city's main street, Damrak, runs from Centraal station to **Dam**, the main square, so called because it was the site of the original dam across the river Amstel for which Amsterdam (originally Amstelledame) was named. Two of the city's most important monuments are on the east side of Dam square, the neo-classical Koninklijk Paleis (Royal Palace), originally built as the town hall, and the Gothic Nieuwekerk (New Church). Damrak splits the oldest part of Amsterdam in two. To the east is Oudezijde (Old Side), full of interesting buildings, but also the heart of the 'red-light' district. To the west is

AMSTERDAM

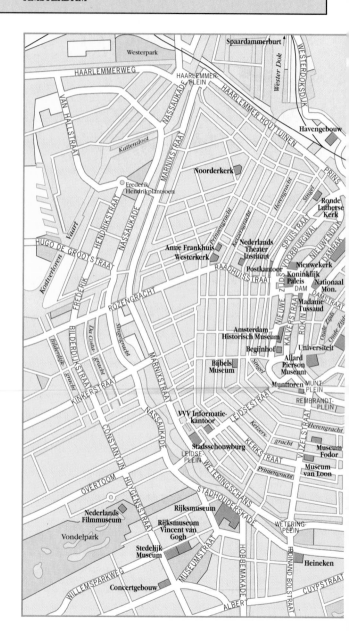

Westerpark

Spaardammerburt

HAARLEMMERWEG

VAN HALLSTRAAT

HAARLEMMER-PLEIN

NASSAUKADE

HAARLEMMER HOUTTUINEN

WESTERDOKSDIJK

Wester Dok

Havengebouw

PRINS

Kattensloot

MARNIXSTRAAT

Noorderkerk

Frederik Hendrikplantsoen

HENDRIKSTRAAT

NASSAUKADE

Prinsengracht

Keizersgracht

Herengracht

Singel

Ronde Lutherse Kerk

HUGO DE GROOT STRAAT

Kostverloren

Vaart

FREDERIK

Anne Frankhuis
Westerkerk

Nederlands Theater Instituut

Postkantoor

RAADHUISSTRAAT

SPUISTRAAT

Nieuwekerk

NIEUWENDIJK

VOORBURGWAL

DAMRAK

Koninklijk Paleis
DAM

Nationaal Mon.

ROZENGRACHT

BILDERDIJKSTRAAT

De Costa gracht

Bilderdijk gracht

Singelgracht

MARNIXSTRAAT

Madame Tussaud

KALVER

Amsterdam Historisch Museum

Begijnhof

Bijbels Museum

Singel

Universiteit

Allard Pierson Museum

ROKIN

Oude Zijds

Oude Zijds

Munttoren MUNT-PLEIN

KINKERSTRAAT

NASSAUKADE

CONSTANTIJN

REMBRANDT-PLEIN

VVV Informatie-kantoor

LEIDSESTRAAT

KERKSTRAAT

Keizers gracht

Herengracht

VIJZELSTRAAT

OVERTOOM

HUYGENSSTRAAT

Stadsschouwburg
LEIDSE-PLEIN

WETERINGSCHANS

Prinsengracht

Museum Fodor

Museum van Loon

STADHOUDERSKADE

Nederlands Filmmuseum

Rijksmuseum

WETERING-PLEIN

Vondelpark

Rijksmuseum Vincent van Gogh

MUSEUMSTRAAT

HOBBEMAKADE

FERDINAND BOL STRAAT

Stedelijk Museum

Heineken

WILLEMSPARKWEG

Concertgebouw

ALBERT

CUYPSTRAAT

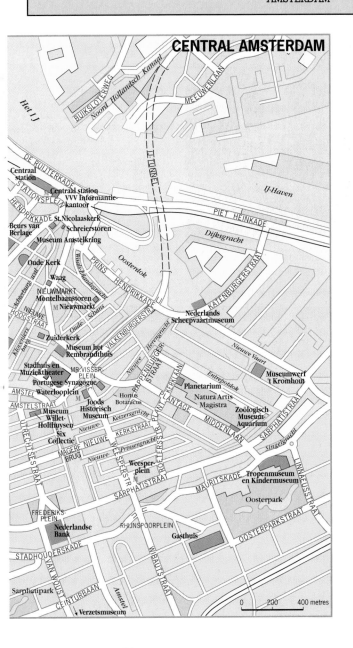

CENTRAL AMSTERDAM

Het IJ

BUIKSLOTERWEG

Noord Hollandsch Kanaal

MEEUWENLAAN

IJ-Haven

DE RUIJTERKADE

Centraal station

STATIONSPLEIN

Centraal station
VVV Informatie-
kantoor

HENDRIKKADE

St. Nicolaaskerk

PIET HEINKADE

Beurs van
Berlage

Schreierstoren

Museum Amstelkring

Dijksgracht

Oosterdok

Oude Kerk

PRINS HENDRIKKADE

Achterburgwal

Waals Eilandsgracht

Waag

KATTENBURGERSTRAAT

NIEUWMARKT

Montelbaanstoren

Nieuwmarkt

Oude Schans

Kloveniers bm

NIEUWE HOOGSTRAAT

Nederlands
Scheepvaartmuseum

Zuiderkerk

VALKENBURGERSTR.

Museum het
Rembrandthuis

Nieuwe

Herengracht

Nieuwe Vaart

Stadhuis en
Muziektheater

MR. VISSER-
PLEIN

RAPENBURGER-
STRAAT

Entrepotdok

Museumwerf
't Kromhout

Portugese Synagogue

Waterlooplein

Planetarium

PLANTAGE

PLANTAGE KERKLAAN

AMSTEL

AMSTELSTRAAT

Hortus
Botanicus

Natura Artis
Magistra

Joods
Historisch
Museum

Keizersgracht

MIDDENLAAN

Zoölogisch
Museum-
Aquarium

Museum
Willet-
Holthuysen

Nieuwe

KERKSTRAAT

ROETERSSTR.

SARPHATISTRAAT

Six
Collectie

MAGERE
BRUG

NIEUWE

Prinsengracht

Singelgracht

Nieuwe

WEESPERSTR.

Weesper-
plein

UTRECHTSESTRAAT

SARPHATISTRAAT

MAURITSKADE

Tropenmuseum
en Kindermuseum

LINNAEUSSTRAAT

Oosterpark

FREDERIKS-
PLEIN

RHIJNSPOORPLEIN

Nederlandse
Bank

Gasthuis

OOSTERPARKSTRAAT

STADHOUDERSKADE

VAN WOUST

Sarphatipark

CEINTURBAAN

Amstel

W. BEUKELSSTRAAT

0   200   400 metres

Verzetsmuseum

Gabled houses on Keizersgracht

Nieuwezijde (New Side), an
area of largely 19th-century
buildings and filled-in canals.
Wrapped around this core is
the horseshoe-shaped
grachtengordel (canal circle)
developed from the
beginning of the 17th century
and lined with handsome
merchants' houses and
warehouses. At the
southernend of the canal
circle is Leidsestraat, a busy
shopping street that leads to
Leidseplein, a bustling square
and the centre of the city's
nightlife, with its theatres,
restaurants and discotheques.
Just south of Leidseplein is the
Museum Quarter, where you
will find the world-famous
Rijksmuseum with its
Rembrandt paintings, the Van
Gogh Museum, the Stedelijk
Museum of modern art and
the up-market shopping
street, PC Hoofstraat. Here too
are many of the city's best-
value hotels.

AMSTERDAMS HISTORISCH MUSEUM
*Entrances at Kalverstraat 92
and Sint Luciensteeg 27*
The Amsterdam Historical
Museum is a must if you want
to understand the history and
development of the city. The
museum occupies the
buildings of the former
Municipal Orphanage,
founded in 1580 and
extended by two leading
17th-century architects,
Hendrik de Keyser and Jacob
van Campen. The buildings
surround quiet cobbled
courtyards where the
orphanage children used to
play. Inside you will find a
mass of maps, paintings and
objects that illustrate the
transformation of Amsterdam
from a simple fishing village
into a major maritime power.
Open: daily 11.00–17.00hrs

ANNE FRANKHUIS
Prinsengracht 263
One of the last entries in Anne
Frank's world-famous diary
reads: 'I want to live on after
my death'. That wish, at least,
has been achieved and the
Anne Frank House now
attracts more than half a
million visitors a year – in
summer it is essential to go
early in the day to avoid long
queues and crowded rooms.
The house is tucked away on
quiet Prinsengracht in the
shadow of Westerkerk's
tower, whose bells are
lyrically described in Anne
Frank's diary. It is a typical
merchant's house, built in

1635, with an *achterhuis*, or back extension, added in 1740, in whose attic the Frank family hid from Nazi persecution from July 1942 until they were arrested in August 1944.

The Anne Frank House remains as it was in 1944, bare of furniture, which was looted after the family was deported. There are magazine pictures of film stars pasted on the wall by Anne and pencil marks recording the heights of the growing sisters. The front of the building is used for exhibitions mounted by the Anne Frank Foundation, which is dedicated to combating prejudice, racism and discrimination in all its forms. *Open:* Jun–Aug, Mon–Sat 09.00–19.00hrs, Sun 10.00–19.00hrs; Sep–May, Mon–Sat 09.00–17.00hrs, Sun 10.00–17.00hrs.

◆
BEGIJNHOF
Entrance at Spui No 14, or from the Amsterdams Historisch Museum
The Begijnhof is a secluded oasis of peace in the bustling heart of the city. The narrow entrance leads into a tree-shaded courtyard surrounded by charming houses. No 34, known as Het Houten Huis (the Wooden House), is the oldest surviving in the city, dating to around 1470.
The Begijnhof was founded in 1346 as a convent for Beguines, women who devoted themselves to charitable work, but without

taking vows of poverty, chastity and obedience. When Catholicism was outlawed in the city they continued to worship in a clandestine chapel hidden behind the façade of No 30. Opposite is the Engelsekerk, the English Church, built in 1727.

◆◆◆
CANAL CIRCLE
One of the highlights of a visit to Amsterdam is a leisurely stroll around the *grachtengordel*, the canal circle, with its houseboats, leafy embankments and stately 17th-century houses. The canal circle represents one of the earliest examples of deliberate town planning in Europe. The scheme was devised by Hendrik Staets, the municipal carpenter, in 1609. His plan involved digging three new canals around the medieval core of the city: the **Herengracht** (Gentlemen's Canal), the **Keizersgracht** (the Emperor's Canal, named after the Holy Roman Emperor, Maximilian I) and the **Prinsengracht** (Prince's Canal, named after Prince William of Orange). Together these canals have a combined length of over 7 miles (12km), if both embankments are included. To pay for the scheme, housing plots were sold to merchants with precisely 100 feet (30m) of frontage, though plots were sometimes subdivided to build smaller houses, or joined together to enable palatial residences to be built.

Shops were only permitted on the narrow interlinking radial canals, which is where they are still found to this day. This policy ensured that the three principal canals present an unbroken vista of domestic houses, individualised by ornate gables and cornices, sculptural reliefs and fine doorcases – spotting the endless variations is part of the fun of a leisurely stroll. Visitors with limited time should concentrate on the part of the canal circle that stretches northwards, towards the harbour, from Raadhuisstraat. Just off this street, on the right, are two of the most unusual canalside houses. The ornate **Bartolotti House** (Herengracht 170–2) is a flamboyant building designed for a wealthy banker by Hendrik de Keyser. The **Netherlands Theater Instituut** (Theatre Museum) next door (No 168) was designed in 1637 by Philips Vingboons; the distinctive 'neck gable', so called because of its resemblance to the neck and shoulders of a

Canal boat tour

wine bottle, was widely copied by other Amsterdam architects. The museum inside this building is worth visiting for its ceiling paintings and displays illustrating the history of Dutch theatre from the 17th century up to the modern age of TV, film and video.

Further along Raadhuisstrat is **Westerkerk** (the West Church), built to Hendrik de Keyser's design in 1623. Its tower, the tallest in Amsterdam at 273 feet (83m), is topped by the gold, red and blue crown of the Habsburg Holy Roman Emperor, Maximilian I. It can be climbed for a bird's eye view of the whole canal circle. From here, heading north along Prinsengracht you will pass the Anne Frankhuis (No 263) and eventually come to **Noorderkerk** (the North Church), built in 1620 to serve the working-class district of Jordaan. On Saturday mornings the square in front of the church hosts the **Boerenmarkt** (Farmers' Market), specialising in organic produce (also a bird market); on Mondays it is the venue for a large bric-a-brac market. At the end of the canal circle you will meet **Brouwersgracht** (the Brewers Canal), one of the most photogenic in the city. The right bank is lined with attractively converted 17th century warehouses, while the canal itself is crossed by numerous bridges. A short way up on the right, in Heremarkt, is **West**

Indischhuis, the headquarters of the West India Company from 1623. Further on, heading back towards the city centre, is the **Ronde Lutherse Kerk** (Lutheran Round Church), a large building with a copper dome, built in 1668. Sheltering beside the church are two attractive step-gabled houses built in 1614 by Hendrik de Keyser – **De Gouden Spiegel** and **De Silveren Spiegel** (the Golden and Silver Mirror). Nearby, at Singel **No 7**, is the smallest house in Amsterdam, only a door's width wide. It is said that the owner built the house like this to avoid property taxes, which were levied according to the length of the façade. From here it is only a short step back to Centraal station.

◆
**HEINEKEN BRAUWERIJ
(Heineken Brewery)**
Stadhouderskade 78
Beer lovers and anyone interested in the social history of brewing will enjoy this excellent museum which charts the invention of beer by the ancient Sumerians, the origins of the first taverns and beer halls in Germany and the role of beer in Carnival festivities as depicted in the paintings of the Brueghels. Audio-visual displays explain the brewing process and the history of Heineken beer, first produced in 1864 and now a household name in many parts of the world. There are guided tours daily during the week.

**KONINKLIJK PALEIS
(Royal Palace)**
Dam
The Royal Palace is Amsterdam's most prestigious architectural monument. It was built between 1648 and 1662, when Amsterdam was at the peak of its power as a maritime trading city, and the sculptures around the pediments express the city's sense of civic pride, with allegorical figures presenting the riches of the earth to the Maid of Amsterdam.
To build such a major structure on the soggy subsoil of mud and silt, the architect, Jacob van Campen, had to create a solid raft of timber piles, each 60 feet (18m) deep. The precise number of the piles – 13,659 – is known to every Amsterdam schoolchild because of a simple formula: to the number of days in the year (365) add 1 in front and 9 behind.
Although originally built as the town hall, the building was turned into a royal palace in 1808 when Napoleon invaded the Netherlands. As a result the interior contains an extensive collection of Empire furniture, but the most striking feature is the wealth of 17th century marble sculpture, the work of Artus Quellin.
Open: summer, daily 13.00–17.00hrs.

MUSEUM AMSTELKRING
Oudezijds Voorburgwal 40
The Amstelkring Museum is also known as *Ons Lieve Heer*

op Solder (Our Lord in the Attic) because there is a beautiful baroque church hidden in the attic, dating from the time when Catholic worship was forbidden in the city. Downstairs, by contrast, is a fine example of a wealthy merchant's residence, built by Jan Hartman in 1661, complete with contemporary furnishings.
Open: Mon–Sat 10.00–17.00hrs, Sun 13.00–17.00hrs.

◆◆
MUSEUM HET REMBRANDTHUIS
Jodenbreestraat 4–6
Rembrandt bought this splendid Renaissance house in 1639 and lived here until 1660 when, having been declared bankrupt, he was forced to move to more modest quarters in the city's Jordaan district. The house is used to display an almost complete set of his etchings – 245 out of the 280 he is known to have made – along with drawings, personal memorabilia and period furniture. One room has an exhibition explaining the techniques of engraving, and the walls are also hung with paintings by Rembrandt's pupils and by his teacher, Pieter Lastman. Rembrandt's own work displays his affection for the low-life characters – beggars, vagabonds, organ grinders and rat catchers – that he saw all around him, living on the edge of the city's poor Jewish quarter.

Open: Mon–Sat 10.00–17.00hrs, Sun 13.00–17.00hrs.

NEDERLANDS SCHEEPVAART MUSEUM (Maritime Museum)
Kattenburgerplein 1
The Dutch Maritime Museum is housed in a massive classical building on the waterfront, which was built in 1656 as the warehouse and arsenal of the Amsterdam Admiralty. This huge building now accommodates several very large historic vessels, as well as evocative paintings and maps and globes, all of which help tell the story of the Dutch maritime achievement. Perhaps the most interesting part of the museum covers the Golden Age and the activities of the East India Company, whose ships plied between the Netherlands and the Spice Islands – modern Indonesia – bringing back the precious cargoes which made Amsterdam extremely prosperous in the 17th century. The subject is brought vividly to life by the sturdy three-masted replica of the East Indiaman *Amsterdam* which is moored in the basin alongside the museum. Children especially love climbing aboard this ship, which gives you a very real sense of the bravery of sailors who plied the oceans in such a vulnerable construction of wood and sailcloth.
Open: Tue–Sat 10.00–17.00hrs, Sun 13.00–17.00hrs.

◆◆◆
RIJKSMUSEUM ✓

Stadhouderskade 42 (tel: (020) 673 2121)

The Rijksmuseum is one of Amsterdam's major highlights. The museum, housed in a vast neo-Gothic palace built in 1885, is far too big to absorb in one visit – it pays to be selective and you can return as often as you like for free if you have a *Museumjaarkaart*, or Museum Card (see **Directory**). Free leaflets showing the layout of the museum are available in the entrance foyer. There is also an informative audio-visual introduction to the art of the Golden Age, with commentaries in several languages, shown at roughly 20-minute intervals in the first floor film theatre.

The museum's most celebrated paintings are displayed on the first floor. They include Rembrandt's *Night Watch*, in Room 224, so called because 19th-century experts believed the painting depicted a night scene. The layers of soot-blackened varnish have since been removed to reveal a quite different picture in which Rembrandt's dramatic use of sunlight and shade can be fully appreciated. Rooms 220 and 223 contain further Rembrandt works, including the arresting *Bridal Pair* (also known as *The Jewish Bride*). Other paintings not be missed in this part of the museum are the works of Frans Hals in Room 209, the witty genre scenes of Jan Steen in Room 216, and the exquisite works of the Delft School hung in Room 222; these include four delightful paintings by Vermeer.

Elsewhere in the museum, the displays in Rooms 101 to 114 illustrate important aspects of Dutch history. Asiatic Art is displayed in the basement, Rooms 11 to 23. Here you will find the arresting figure of Shiva, Lord of the Dance, surrounded by a ring of fire, a stunning 12th century bronze from southern India. The Sculpture and Applied Art collection, Rooms 238 to 261, includes statues rescued from churches in the Netherlands, and a large collection of Delftware. Equally popular are the dolls' houses in Room 162, made in the 18th century. The remaining rooms illustrate Dutch interior design from the 18th to the early 20th century.

Open: Tue–Sat 10.00–17.00hrs, Sun 13.00–17.00hrs.

The Rijksmuseum

♦♦♦
RIJKSMUSEUM VINCENT VAN GOGH ✓

Paulus Potterstraat 7

Van Gogh's artistic career lasted a mere ten years, yet he painted over 2000 works in that time. This collection, consisting of some 200 paintings and 600 drawings, was bequeathed to the city by Van Gogh's nephew. The work is presented in chronological order, beginning with his early studies of peasant life painted in 1884–5 and ending with the tortured paintings that he produced in 1889–90, just before his suicide. Paintings from his time in Arles are the highlight of the collection: they are extraordinarily vivid and intense and the colours are stunning – the blazing yellows and oranges of sunflowers, the brilliant white of peach blossom against a turquoise spring sky, the blues and yellows of harvest scenes all speak of his enthusiasm for 'the full effect of colour'.

Open: Tue–Sat 10.00–17.00hrs, Sun 13.00–17.00hrs.

Zoo encounter

♦
ZOO (ARTIS)

Plantage Kerklaan 40

Amsterdam's zoo opened in 1838 under the grand title of Natura Artis Magister (Nature, Teacher of the Arts). Now known simply as Artis, the zoo offers enough attractions to fill the best part of a day. As well as 6,000 animals kept in naturalistic enclosures, there is a children's farm, a spectacular planetarium, a tropical house and a large aquarium. The ticket includes admission to two museums on the site – the **Geologisch Museum**, illustrating the earth's evolution, and the **Zoologisch Museum**, whose tableaux and audio-visuals explain the characteristic flora and fauna of the country.

Open: daily 09.00–17.00hrs.

Accommodation

Ambassade, Herengracht 341 (tel: (020) 626 2333). Three-star, 46 rooms; a very comfortable bed and breakfast hotel in a row of 17th-century canal houses.

Asterisk, Den Texstraat 14–16 (tel: (020) 626 2396). Two-star, 19 rooms; a simple, inexpensive hotel in a quiet residential district near the Rijksmuseum.

Canal House, Keizersgracht 148 (tel: (020) 622 5182). Three-star, 26 rooms; an unusual 17th-century merchant's house on the canal – full of character.

Doelen Karena, Nieuwe Doelenstraat 24 (tel: (020) 622 0722). Four-star, 85 rooms; a 17th-century building with ornate external decoration, and a comfortable old-fashioned feel. The following centrally located, four-star hotels are all part of the same reliable group: **Caransa Karena**, Rembrandtplein 19 (tel: (020) 622 9455); **Rembrandt Karena**, Herengracht 255 (tel: (020) 622 1727) and **Schiller Karena**, Rembrandtplein 26–36 (tel: (020) 623 1660). **Grand**, Oudezijds Voorburgwal 197 (tel: (020) 555 3111). Five-star, 170 rooms, a brand new luxury hotel in the former Admiralty building, close to the university quarter. **Hotel de l'Europe**, Nieuwe Doelenstraat 2–8 (tel: (020) 623 4836). Five-star, 101 rooms; old-fashioned grandeur at a price. **Pulitzer**, Prinsengracht 315–331 (tel: (020) 523 5235). Five-star, 236 rooms, a beautifully designed conversion of a block of 17th-century canal houses with gardens, the most original hotel in the city.

Eating Out

Amsterdam has a great range of restaurants in all price brackets, and the majority are pleasantly informal and inexpensive.
Casa da David, Singel 426 (tel: (020) 624 5093). Home-made pasta with inventive sauces, and first-rate pizza cooked in a wood-fired oven. Inexpensive.
China Treasure, Nieuwezijds Voorburgwal 115 (tel: (020) 626 0915). Luxurious

restaurant employing specialist master chefs for each of its regional cuisines – Cantonese, Peking and Szechuan. Excellent lunchtime *dim sum*. Moderate to expensive.
Dynasty, Reguliersdwars-straat 30 (tel: (020) 626 8400). Smart and fashionable, with a modern oriental decor. Highly original dishes combining elements of Cantonese, Thai, Vietnamese and Indonesian cuisine. Moderate to expensive.
Excelsior, Hotel de l'Europe, Nieuwe Doelenstraat 2–8 (tel: (020) 623 4863). Grand Michelin-starred restaurant with panoramic views over the river Amstel. Seafood and game specialities and a comprehensive wine list. Expensive.
Filoxenia, Berenstraat 8 (tel: (020) 624 4292). Small and friendly Greek restaurant serving succulent herb-flavoured kebabs at reasonable prices.
De Gouden Reael, Zandhoek 14 (tel: (020) 623 3883). Authentic regional French cuisine, served with friendliness and flair. Inexpensive set menus.
Hotel Die Port van Cleve, Nieuwezijds Voorburgwal 178–80 (tel: (020) 624 0047). Two restaurants in this venerable old hotel: De Blauwe Parade, renowned for the old Delftware picture tiles on its walls, and the slightly cheaper De Poort. Authentic Dutch dishes, such as split-pea soup (*erwtensoep*), plus excellent steaks.

De Kersentuin, Garden Hotel, Dijsselhofplantsoen 7 (tel: (020) 664 2121). The 'Cherry Orchard' is one of the most prestigious restaurants in the Netherlands, famed for the imaginative dishes of Jon Sistermans, who combines oriental flavours and presentational flair with traditional ingredients. Expensive.

Koh-I-Noor, Westermarkt 29 (tel: (020) 623 3133). Popular restaurant serving all the classic northern Indian dishes plus inexpensive meat and vegetarian thali set menus.

Lucius, Spuistraat 247 (tel: (020) 624 1831). Old-fashioned establishment serving the best fresh fish and seafood in Amsterdam. Moderate to expensive.

Orient, Van Baelestraat 21 (tel: (020) 673 9428). A good choice if you are not familiar with Indonesian cuisine – the helpful menu explains the various dishes that make up a traditional *rijsttafel* banquet. The Wednesday self-service buffet is a popular and inexpensive way of sampling the complete range.

Popocatepetl, Nieuwezijds Voorburgwal 163–165 (tel: (020) 662 4541). Lively restaurant, top-class margueritas and refreshing Mexican beer served in an ice bucket with lime. All the standard Mexican dishes plus popular spare ribs with thick fried chips.

Rum Runners, Prinsengracht 277 (tel: (020) 627 4079). Young, fun café with tropical decor, renowned for its

cocktails; outdoor eating in summer. Spicy fish stews and cooling salads plus vegetarian options and Tex-Mex. Live music on Wednesday to Sunday afternoons. Moderate prices.

Speciaal, Nieuwe Leliestraat 142 (tel: (020) 624 9706). A semi-tropical gourmet paradise tucked away in the Jordaan district with a loyal band of regular patrons who maintain that this is Amsterdam's best Indonesian restaurant. Moderate to expensive.

't Swarte Schaep Korte Leidsedwarsstraat 24 (tel: (020) 622 3021). The 'Black Sheep' maintains the highest culinary standards whilst remaining relatively inexpensive. Even members of the Dutch royal family come here for the subtle blend of traditional French and Dutch cuisine and for the characterful timbered interior of the 300-year old building.

Entertainment
Amsterdam's lively entertainments scene caters for every taste. For a complete listing of events that can be enjoyed by non-Dutch speakers look for the magazine *What's on in Amsterdam*, available at the VVV tourist office and at many hotels.

Classical music, ballet and opera
Concerts given by the **Royal Concertgebouw Orchestra**, under conductor Riccardo Chailly are always a treat, but advance booking is advisable.

The **Muziektheater** (at Amstel 3), part of the controversial modern Stopera development, is home to the Nederlandse Opera and the Nationale Ballet. The Nederlandse Dans Theater puts in occasional guest performances of modern choreography. Musicians from the Opera and Ballet orchestras give free lunchtime concerts in summer. The **Beurs van Berlage** (Damrak 219–41), Amsterdam's former stock and commodities exchange, is now a cultural centre, home to the Netherlands Philharmonic and Chamber Orchestras.

Nightlife

Jazz

The **Bimhuis** (Oude Schans 72) run by BIM, the jazz musicians' union, is rated one of Europe's best venues and attracts top performers from all over the world. Concerts are given on Thursday, Friday and Saturday nights. **Joseph Lam's Jazzclub**, located in the western docks area, is packed every Saturday night with fans of traditional and Dixieland jazz.

Rock music

Amsterdam has two top venues which, though small, still attract top-name bands; the atmosphere at both is refreshingly relaxed, with no dress code. **Melkweg** (Milky

Way), at Lijnbaansgracht 234A, so called because it is located in a converted dairy, features world music, reggae, African, South American and roots music. **Paradiso**, located in a converted church on Weteringschans, offers the same mix as Melkweg.

Cinema

Amsterdam has numerous commercial cinemas, but the best is **Tuschinski** (at Reguliersbreestraat 26–8), worth visiting just for its beautiful and authentic 1920s interior. This is Amsterdam's showcase cinema used for celebrity premieres. Expect queues at weekends if you have not booked in advance. For art movies and cinema classics head for the **Nederlands Filmmuseum**, in Vondelpark. This shows three different films a day and the terrace is used for outdoor screenings in summer.

Shopping

Amsterdam has scores of small speciality shops dotted all round the canal circle which you will discover by browsing, or by getting hold of the useful shopping guides published by the VVV tourist office.

The main department stores are located on **Dam** square; here you will find De Bijenkorf (The Beehive), known as the Harrods of Amsterdam, C & A (No 75) and Peek & Cloppenburg. **Kalverstraat**, the main shopping street, runs from Dam square to Muntplein. Here you will find plenty of bargain clothes

shops and several well-known chain stores, such as the American Discount Book Center (No 185), Marks & Spencer (at the corner of Sint Luciensteeg), Body Shop (at Nos 157–9), and W H Smith (at No 152) which has a comprehensive guidebook section covering Amsterdam and the Netherlands. At the junction of Kalverstraat and Spui is the splendid Empire-style building occupied by the fashion chain, Esprit. On **Muntplein**, alongside the Munttoren, is De Porceleyne Fles, the official outlet for genuine hand-painted Delftware, marked on the base with the letter D – a considerably superior product to the cheap mass-produced pottery sold as Delft in many souvenir shops. A few steps away, on Singel, is the **Bloemenmarkt** (Flower Market), where florists sell bulbs, seeds, floral bouquets and even clipped box topiary from floating stalls. The florists here can arrange shipping for you.

On nearby **Leidsestraat** you will find Metz & Co, which sells the products of top international designers – furniture, fabrics, kitchenware, glass and smaller gift items such as ornaments and toiletries. The striking post-modernist café on the top floor is a good place to rest your feet and enjoy fine views. Not far from the Rijksmuseum is the **Spiegelkwartier**, renowned for its concentration of antique shops, where you can pick up relatively inexpensive Dutch tiles or spend a fortune on an Old Master. In Nieuwe Spiegelstraat, Kunsthandel Aalderink, No 15, specialises in oriental and ethnographic art, F G Glebbing, No 70, has a good stock of furniture, Kunsthandel Frans Leidelmeijer, No 58, specialises in art deco glass, lamps, statues and ceramics, and the Amsterdam Antiques Gallery, No 34, has ten dealers under one roof, selling icons, clocks, pewter, paintings and scientific instruments amongst other things.

The prices are slightly lower in **Kerstraat** where De Haas, No 155, specialises in art nouveau and art deco, and Lambiek, No 78, sells thousands of antique comics and the original drawings of comic artists and cartoonists.

Markets

No visit to Amsterdam would be complete without a visit to the huge market in **Albert Cuypstraat** (Mon–Sat 09.00–17.00hrs), a crowded, colourful and vibrant affair attended by up to 50,000 people on a typical Saturday – 5 per cent of the city's population. The stalls and milling crowds stretch for nearly a mile, making this Europe's biggest general market. Even if you do not intend to buy, you will be entertained by stalls piled high with exotic fish and vegetables, colourful cheeses and bolts of fabric, and the passing parade of people of

Waterlooplein market

all the races that make up this multi-ethnic city. Amsterdam's other big market, on **Waterlooplein** (Mon–Fri 10.00–17.00hrs, Sat 08.30–17.30hrs) sells all sorts of bric-a-brac – fun to browse, and bargaining over the price is all part of the fun.

Diamonds

Amsterdam has been an important centre for diamond processing since the 17th century. The following long-established companies offer tours of their workshops where you can see diamond cutters and polishers at work turning rough stones into sparkling gems: **Amsterdam Diamond Center**, Rokin 1–5; **Van Moppes Diamonds**, Albert Cuypstraat 2–6; **Coster Diamonds**, Paulus Potterstraat 2–6; **Gassan Diamonds**, Nieuwe Vilenburgerstraat 173–175.

AROUND AMSTERDAM

Amsterdam makes the perfect base for a series of whole or half-day excursions into the attractive countryside nearby. All the sights detailed below are accessible by train or bus, and numerous tour operators offer inexpensive coach excursions (details from your hotel or the Amsterdam VVV tourist office).

AALSMEER BLOEMENVEILINGEN (Flower Auction)

Legmeerdijk 313, Aalsmeer, 9 miles (16km) southwest
This is the world's biggest cut-flower market and makes for a fascinating visit, but you must be an early riser; to see the best of the auctions it is advisable to be there at about 8am. If you can manage that, you'll miss the tour buses. The auction hall is huge, with a viewing gallery for visitors above the market area. From here you can see both the sea of flowers and the rapid pace of the auction. Taped commentaries in various languages will explain this extraordinary spectacle and provide you with an inside look at the workings of the Dutch flower trade.

◆◆
ALKMAAR

22 miles (37km) northwest
Alkmaar is well worth a visit for its cheese market (*open*: mid Apr–mid Sept, Fri 10.00–12.00hrs), which is run along rigidly traditional lines. White-garbed porters, wearing the badge of the ancient cheese trade guild, carry the yellow-and red-waxed cheeses to the Waag (Weigh-house) and from there to the many cheese stalls. The **Kaasmuseum** (Cheese Museum) on the upper floor of the Waag gives an interesting account of the process of cheese-making, and the town itself has many attractive buildings.

AVIODOME

Schiphol Centrum
If you are flying out of the Netherlands from Schiphol airport it may be worth going a little early and visiting this interesting aviation museum. The exhibits show the history of Dutch aviation, along with developments in aviation technology from the earliest aircraft to modern capsules. Children will particularly enjoy the opportunity to step inside the cockpit of a real aeroplane. *Open*: Mon–Fri 10.00–17.00hrs, Sat–Sun 12.00–17.00hrs.

EDAM

12 miles (20km) northeast
Edam is a surprisingly unspoilt town, despite the worldwide fame of its cheeses. These are made in factories and farms in the surrounding countryside and sold in many varieties at the traditional cheese market (held on Wednesday mornings in summer) as well as in several specialist shops.
Edam is a fine example of an archetypal Dutch town, with numerous little bridges criss-crossing the canals. Walking around the centre you can see the old **Kaasmarkt** (Cheese

Market) and **Waag** (Weigh-house), which houses an informative exhibition about the history of Edam's cheese-making. On the main square, look out for the **Stadhuis** (Town Hall) with its ornate internal and external decoration. The **Edams Museum** on the same square is full of interesting local information and has an unusual floating cellar. In season the fine 15th-century Gothic **Grote Kerk** (Great Church) is open in the afternoons – the beautiful stained glass windows and the details of the choir are worth seeing.

Accommodation

De Fortuna, Spuistraat 1–7 (tel: (02993) 71671). Three-star, 30 rooms, a charming, friendly hotel on the canal; bed and breakfast only, but there are several restaurants in the town.

Alkmaar's cheese market

◆◆◆
ENKHUIZEN ✓

28 miles (45km) northeast
The main reason for visiting Enkuizen is for the excellent **Zuiderzeemuseum**. Until the Afsluitdijk was built in 1932, effectively blocking off the Zuiderzee (now the IJsselmeer) from the North Sea, Enkhuizen was an important and prosperous sea port. The Dutch government set about creating the museum here in order to show future generations what life was like before the Zuiderzee was dammed off. The museum was finally completed in 1983, and it is an outstanding achievement. There are two parts to the museum – the **Buitenmuseum** (outdoor museum, open: daily, mid Apr–late Oct 10.00-17.00hrs) and the **Binnenmuseum** (indoor

Enkhuizen's open-air museum

museum, *open*: daily 10.00–17.00hrs). The only way of getting to the outdoor museum is by boat, and this is well sign-posted. A complete Zuiderzee village – around 140 houses – has been reconstructed by bringing houses and workshops, brick by brick, from all over the area, building streets and canals to ensure authenticity. The most acute attention to detail has been observed in this faithful reproduction of life as it was in the Zuiderzee fishing ports from the 1880s to 1930s.

The indoor museum is full of boats that have sailed on the Zuiderzee, wooden figure-heads, anchors, fishing nets – everything, in fact, to do with fishing, shipping and related trades. It also includes traditional local costumes and furniture.

◆◆◆
HAARLEM
8 miles (5km) west
The main sights of this dignified small town, the capital of Noord Holland, lie in and close to the main square, **Grote Markt**. On the square itself are three imposing buildings. The **Grote Kerk** (also known as St Bavokerk) dominates the south side with its 15th-century wooden lantern tower rising to over 262 feet (80m). Alongside the church is the **Vleeshal** (Meat Market), built in 1603 and ornately decorated with ox-head motifs. It is now used to house temporary art exhibitions. To the west of the square is Haarlem's ancient Stadhuis (Town Hall), an imposing Gothic building started in the 14th century and extended in the Renaissance period.

If you leave the square by the southeastern exit, down Damstraat, you will come to the embankment of the River Spaarne. A little way up, on the left, is the entrance to the **Teylers Museum**. This is believed to be the first museum ever to open in the Netherlands. Pieter Teyler left a bequest to promote interest in the sciences and the arts, and to this end the museum was established on his death in 1778. Particularly worth seeing is the vast collection of 16th to 19th-century drawings from all over Europe.

From the Teylers Museum you should retrace your steps to Grote Markt, then head south between Grote Kerk and the Vleeshal, following Warmoestraat, Schagchelstraat and Groot Heiligland. This will bring you to Haarlem's star attraction, the **Frans Halsmuseum**.

Born in Antwerp, Frans Hals came to live in Haarlem with his family in 1591 (he was then about ten years old). He established himself as a portrait painter and scarcely ventured beyond Haarlem for the rest of his life, earning his living by painting the successful and influential people of the town. Sadly, near the end of his life, Frans Hals became an impoverished inmate of the same old people's home which now houses this wonderful collection of his work. His last portraits took on a gloomy air, but even in solemnity the portraits are unforgettable. Apart from the works of Frans Hals, this museum houses a varied collection of paintings by other 17th-century masters, particularly of the Haarlem school. The modern collection is also interesting, and there are temporary exhibitions of modern sculpture.

◆
HOORN
27 miles (43km) north
Hoorn was once a very prosperous sea-port on the Zuiderzee, until its access to the open sea was blocked off by the construction of the Afsluitdijk dam in 1932. Now it is predominantly a port for pleasure boats. It was also famous for weaving huge herring nets, and even today fishing nets hang drying from the traditional sailing barges anchored in the harbour. The harbour is a beautiful spot and its embankment, the **Veermanskade**, is lined with well-restored merchants' houses and some interesting old warehouses. There are some cafés and restaurants here too which provide good vantage points for watching the boating activity and counting the herons who wait patiently for the next fishing boat to return. The squat **Hoofdtoren** was originally built as a watch tower for the entrance to the port; it is now joined by a modern sculpture of a group of children, and the upper floor is a restaurant. The **Westfries Museum** has a mixed collection of interesting items and furniture, but it is the flamboyant baroque façade that should not be missed. The shops are good and there are a number of sophisticated cafés dotted about town.

Accommodation
De Magneet, Kleine Oost 5–7 (tel: (02290) 15021). Three-star, 46 rooms, nearest the harbour.

Eating Out
De Oude Rosmolen (Fonk), Duinsteeg 1 (tel: (02290) 14752). A small, characterful restaurant serving inventive French-influenced cuisine.

◆◆◆
KEUKENHOF AND LISSE ✓

12 miles (18km) south
The huge flower gardens at Keukenhof, near the town of Lisse, form a superb showcase for the Dutch bulb industry. The 70-acre (28-ha) park is a sea of beautiful blooms and strong colours during the short bulb season. Despite its size, the garden can also seem completely packed with visitors, especially at weekends, since people travel from all over Europe for the sight. There is a huge indoor garden, and the rest of the park is divided by canals and paths where you can wander amidst thousands of crocuses, tulips, daffodils and hyacinths. It is possible to buy bulbs from the Keukenhof shop to take away or have sent to your home. Returning north from Lisse in the direction of Haarlem there is a beautiful drive through the bulb district where commercial horticulturists raise the stock. The daffodils and tulips are allowed to bloom just long enough to enable the growers to check the variety and ensure they are free from disease. After that the flowers are mown off so that all the plant's energy goes into producing new side bulbs – hence the piles of discarded flowers you will often see lying by the roadside.
Open: end Mar–end May, 08.00–20.00hrs.

◆◆
MARKEN, MONNICKENDAM AND VOLENDAM
10 miles (16km) north
Heading north from Amsterdam a well-worn tourist route takes

Vivid blooms at Keukenhof

in the three pretty villages of Marken, Monnickendam and Volendam. On your way take time to stop in Broek-in-Waterland, a charming and incredibly neat village set beside a lake with a fine church, a shoe factory and a model cheese dairy.

Monnickendam is less touristy than Marken or Volendam and worth a quick look around; it has an attractive harbour and some finely gabled houses in the main street.

Volendam, by contrast, is completely geared to tourists; local people wear traditional costume and pose for photographs, souvenirs hang outside every shop round the harbour, and the tiny former fishing village can become stifled with coachloads of trippers. This is a pity because the small town and harbour is very pretty, with most of the characterful wooden houses tucked down behind a huge dyke keeping the sea back. You can take a boat from here to **Marken**, which is quite sleepy by comparison with its neighbour. Marken was an island until it was linked to the mainland by a causeway in 1957, and it still has an island feel. Today it has the appearance of a model village with brightly painted, pretty houses, a quiet harbour and a handful of cafés and restaurants.

◆◆
MUIDEN

5 miles (8km) southeast
The main attraction here is the moated castle, called the

Muiderslot. Originally built in the 13th century, the castle had to be rebuilt a century later after it was destroyed by the Bishop of Utrecht. It suffered further over the centuries and was only saved from total demolition at the end of the last century. The castle had fallen into considerable disrepair since the time of the poet and historian, Pieter Hooft, who looked after it from 1609–47. He had encouraged literary, musical and intellectual gatherings at the castle, and those involved became known as the Muiderkring (the Muiden Circle). The castle has now been beautifully restored and furnished as it would have been during Hooft's occupation. There are pleasant lawns and gardens around the moat.

NAARDEN

12 miles (20km) southeast
Approached through the pretty woodland district of Gooi, and close to the bird sanctuary on Lake Naarden, this is an excellent example of a fortress city, with moats and ramparts and an attractive old town centre. The interesting **Vestingmuseum** (Fortification Museum) is housed in one of the ramparts and explains the history and workings of the town's defence system. Another small museum, at Turfpoortstraat 27, is devoted to the memory of the Czech educational theorist, John Comenius, who died here. The tourist office suggests a number of walking tours to get the best from your visit.

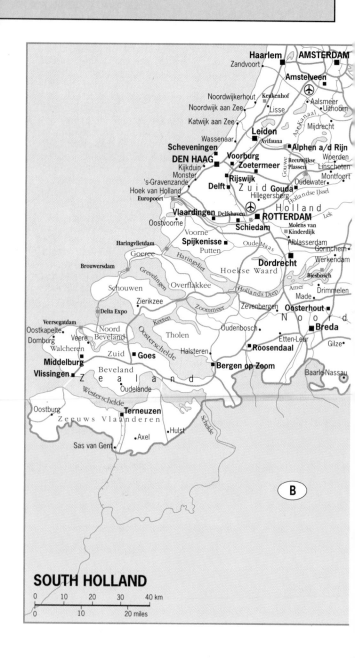

SOUTH HOLLAND

0   10   20   30   40 km
0   10   20 miles

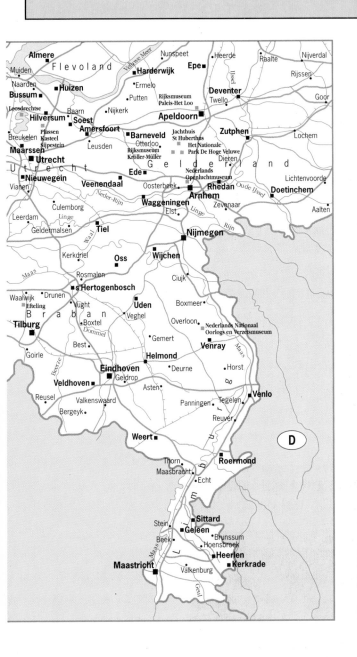

ZUID HOLLAND

The province of Zuid (South) Holland is one of the most influential in the Netherlands. Its cities – Rotterdam, Den Haag (The Hague), Leiden and Dordrecht are commercially, economically and culturally of major importance within the country. The ports along the Maas river, which links to the Rijn (Rhine), are central to trading in Europe and the river itself has been a crucial communications and transport link for centuries.

DELFT

Delft is a charming and beautiful town located 7 miles (11km) from Rotterdam and 5 miles (8km) from Den Haag, its canals crossed by bridges and lined with fine merchants' houses. Cobbled streets link the network of waterways and the town has a charm not found in its larger neighbours. A well-respected university town, Delft has both scholastic and cultural status and makes an attractive base for exploring the region. It can, however, become

Souvenirs of Delft

extremely busy in the high season. Canal cruises and horse-drawn carriage tours both offer pleasant ways of seeing the town in summer. Although its origins go back to the 11th century, large areas of Delft were destroyed by fire in 1536 and most of the buildings of note were subsequently rebuilt. In the 13th and 14th centuries the city's economy was based on the production of cloth and beer. A waterway was built to link the city with the mouth of the River Maas to facilitate the export of these products; a new port was established, Delfshaven, which remained under the jurisdiction of Delft until it was incorporated into the city of Rotterdam in 1886.

Sons of Delft include Hugo de Groot (1583–1645), also known as Grotius, famous for his scholarly works which laid the foundations for international law, and Jan Vermeer (1632–75) who founded the Delft school of painting. Although Vermeer was virtually unknown in his lifetime, he is now considered one of the great masters of the Netherlands. Most of his paintings of Delft and scenes from everyday life are to be found in the Rijksmuseum in Amsterdam and the Mauritshuis in Den Haag.

Production of the world-famous blue and white pottery, called Delftware, began in the 16th century when local potters began to copy imported Chinese porcelain. The local industry reached its height in the 18th century but nearly collapsed when cheap, mass-produced pottery from England began to flood the market. By the mid 19th century there was only one factory left specialising in the art of hand-painted Delftware. That factory – De Porceleyne Fles – is still in production and can be visited (see below).

DE PORCELEYNE FLES (The Porcelain Jar)
Rotterdamseweg 196
Established in 1653, this is the town's oldest surviving Delftware factory. Traditional methods of production are still used and every detail of the blue-glaze decoration is painted by hand. Each piece is thus unique, and comes with a certificate of authenticity. Visitors can watch potters and artists at work and buy traditional and modern pieces in the factory showroom.

◆◆
HET PRINSENHOF
Sint Agathaplein 1
This building started life as the convent of St Agatha, before William the Silent made it his campaign headquarters during the Dutch Revolt against Spanish rule. He took up residence here in 1572, but was assassinated by a fanatical Catholic in 1585 in the sombre room on the first floor called the Moordzaal (Death Room). The convent is now a museum with exhibitions of paintings, tapestries, silverware and various objects dealing with the history of Delft.
Open: Tue–Sat 10.00–17.00hrs, Sun 13.00–17.00hrs.

MUSEUM LAMBERT VAN MEERTEN
Oude Delft 199
This 19th-century mansion has a fine display of furnishings set in beautifully panelled rooms. The high spot is the collection of 17th and early 18th-century hand-painted Delftware tiles. These are displayed in the large hallway, up the stairs and on the landings, and each selection is labelled with a description of the origins of the patterns used. Look out for the particularly appealing Cupid tile collection.
Open: Tue–Sat 10.00–17.00hrs, Sun 13.00–17.00hrs.

◆◆
NIEUWE KERK (New Church)
Markt
New in 1381, this Gothic church has a plain interior but its size is impressive. The stained glass windows are modern (by Joep Nicolas); one is a tribute to Hugo Grotius, the Delft-born lawyer whose bronze statue stands outside the church. The most memorable feature of the church is the huge tomb of William of Orange. Carved out of black and white marble, this dominates the choir. It took nearly ten years to complete and the sarcophagus is surrounded by large allegorical figures.
In summer visitors can climb the tower for excellent views of the town. The tower's bell carillon, created by the Hemony brothers in the 17th century, is magnificent and the sound echoes throughout the streets on the hour.

◆
OUDE KERK (Old Church)
Heilige Geestkerkhof
This church, with its leaning tower, was begun around 1240 and extended several times up to the 16th century. Inside are the tombs of Dutch naval heroes, dignitaries and artists, including that of Vermeer.

Accommodation
Delft is inundated by tourists in summer when it is essential to book in advance. The tourist office has lists of hotels, guesthouses and rooms to rent.
De Ark, Koormarkt 65 (tel: (015) 157999). Four-star, 16 rooms, a small, cosy and central hotel overlooking the canal.
Delft Museumhotel, Oude Delft 189 (tel: (015) 140930). Four-star, 51 rooms; a comfortable central hotel in two well-preserved 17th-century houses.

Eating Out
De Zwethheul, Rotterdamseweg 480 (tel: (015) 470 4166). Good views and excellent food, but not cheap and some way from the town.
L'Escalier, Oude Delft 125 (tel: (015) 124621). Delicious *nouvelle cuisine* in the setting of an old canal-side house.
De Prensenkelder, Schoolstraat 11 (tel: (015) 121860). Very atmospheric restaurant in the vaulted cellars of the Prinsenhof museum.
Le Vieux Jean, Heilige Geestkerkhof 3 (tel: (015) 130433). Simple but stylish French restaurant.
Stads-Koffyhuis, Oude Delft 133 (tel (015) 124625). Cheerful students' café serving huge, well-stuffed pancakes.

DEN HAAG

The Hague, as it is known in English, is the seat of the Dutch government, the official residence of Queen Beatrix and

an international centre for diplomacy. The predominance of 18th and 19th-century houses give the wide streets a particular elegance and dignity. At the heart of The Hague is the Binnenhof, a group of buildings in which the two chambers of the Dutch parliament hold their debates. The buildings of the Binnenhof are reflected to the north, in the tranquil waters of

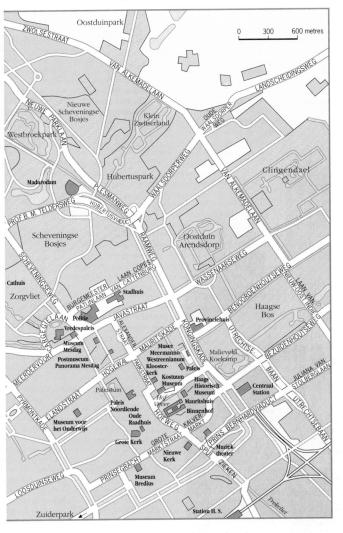

Hof Vijver, a small lake which once formed part of a moat. In the immediate environs there are stately houses, quiet cobbled courtyards and elegant shopping streets. Chic shops around the Oude Kerk (Old Church) cater for the international business and diplomatic community as well as residents. Further out there are numerous museums and parks, while the seaside resort of Scheveningen is a mere 2 miles (3km) away.

◆

BINNENHOF
Entrance from Buitenhof
The Hague owes its origins to a castle built in 1250 by William II, the Count of Holland. The Binnenhof is the inner courtyard of that ancient castle, and a statue of Count William II stands just by the entrance. The main building at the centre of the courtyard is the **Ridderzaal** (Knights' Hall), a restored 13th-century building in which the two chambers of the Dutch parliament meet on special occasions. The grandest of these occasions takes place on the third Tuesday in September, when the Queen arrives in full ceremony in a golden coach, approaching from the Noordeinde Palace on the Lange Voorhout. Parliament then gathers in the central Gothic hall to hear the Queen's speech, setting out the government's plans for the coming year. An exhibition in the vaults of the Ridderzaal explains the formal structures of government in the Netherlands and the responsibilities of the two chambers.
Open: Mon–Sat 10.00–16.00hrs; Jul–Aug also Sun 12.00–16.00hrs.

◆◆

HAAGS GEMEENTEMUSEUM
Stadhouderslaan 41
The Hague Municipal Museum was designed in 1935 by the renowned Dutch architect, H P Berlage, in art deco style. The high spot of the museum is the

Utrecht's cathedral tower in miniature at Madurodam

extraordinary collection of musical instruments from around the world. The best way of appreciating the range of these instruments and their different sounds is to rent a tape recorder at the entrance and listen to the 50-minute commentary as you go round. Much of the museum is devoted to an excellent collection of works by 19th and 20th-century artists, including paintings by Piet Mondriaan, and Impressionist works by artists of the Hague School. One gallery is devoted to costume, and others include displays of glass, gold and silverware, Islamic and Chinese ceramics and period furniture.
Open: Tue–Sun 11.00–17.00hrs.

◆
MADURODAM
Haringkade 175
This is the Netherlands in miniature: buildings and landscapes from all over the country are reproduced here in precise detail at one twenty-fifth of their actual size. Visitors may well recognise particular houses or streets from Amsterdam and Den Haag. Rotterdam's Europoort and Schiphol airport are included, as well as bulb fields and windmills. After dark the town is illuminated by around 50,000 lights, and on July and August evenings a fairytale sound and light show ('Moonlight Miracle') entrances young and old alike.
Open: late Mar–May, daily 09.00–22.30hrs; Jun–Aug, 09.00–23.00hrs; Sep, 09.00–21.30hrs; Oct–early Jan, 09.00–18.00hrs.

◆◆◆
MAURITSHUIS ✓

Korte Vijverberg 8
This is considered to be one of the finest art galleries of its size in the world. The serene building was commissioned by Prince John Maurice of Nassau in the 17th century, hence the name Mauritshuis. The architect was Jacob van Campen, and the building epitomises the assured elegance of the Golden Age. Inside are hung paintings of the Flemish School, Dutch masterpieces from the Golden Age and a number from foreign schools, including Rubens, Holbein the Younger, Frans Hals, Rembrandt and Vermeer are represented here. Amongst outstanding paintings here is Paulus Potter's *The Young Bull*.
Open: Tue–Sat 10.00–17.00hrs, Sun 11.00–17.00hrs.

A pastoral scene in the Mauritshuis

◆

MESDAG MUSEUM
Laan van Meerdervoort 7F
H W Mesdag, a leading painter
of the Dutch Impressionist
Hague School, had this house
built especially for his collection
in 1869. He left it to the nation
on his death in 1915. The
collection is well worth seeing
and provides an opportunity to
compare the seascapes painted
by Mesdag and his
contemporaries with
landscapes painted by
members of the French
Barbizon School – artists such
as Corot and Millet.
Open: Tue–Sat 10.00–17.00hrs,
Sun 13.00–17.00hrs.

◆

MUSEON
Stadhouderslaan 41
The Museon stands next door to
the Haags Gemeentemuseum
but offers a totally different
experience. This is a very
modern museum, with large-
scale exhibits covering a range
of subjects from the
fundamentals of science to the
way of life of different peoples
of the earth. The museum is
well laid out with bright
graphics, lots of glass and
shining metalwork, and groups
of school-children adding to the
general noise level.
The Museon aims to be
educative but fun, and one area
dedicated to computers and
telephones encourages visitors
to participate, pressing buttons
and seeing themselves on TV
screens. A natural history
display shows a section through
a typical Dutch sand-dune
landscape, accompanied by the
sound of the wind, showing how
the movement of the sea effects
the sand formations.
Open: Tue–Sat 10.00–17.00hrs,
Sun 13.00–17.00hrs.

◆◆

PANORAMA MESDAG
Zeestraat 65B
The Panorama Mesdag is an
extraordinary experience, not
to be missed. Climbing up a
wooden spiral staircase the
visitor emerges on an open
bandstand platform from
where, spread out over a 360
degree canvas, 394 feet (111m)
in circumference and 46 feet
(14m) high, the seaside resort
of Scheveningen is laid out to
view, painted with remarkable
realism as it was in 1880. The
effect is entrancing: it feels as
though you were actually
standing among the sand
dunes, looking out to sea in one
direction and into the town on
the other. The artist, H W
Mesdag, with a carefully
chosen team (including his
wife) sketched out the
panorama and managed to
paint it in the astonishing time of
four months.
Open: Mon–Sat 10.00–17.00hrs,
Sun 12.00–17.00hrs.

◆

PARKS
Clingendael Park (entrance
from Wassenaarsweg) has a
beautiful Japanese garden
(*open:* May–mid June), well
worth visiting. **Zuider Park**, on
the south side of the town, has
many family attractions
including a swimming pool,
recreation centre, zoo, bird-
park, children's farm and a
miniature steam railway.

◆
SCHEVENINGEN

The seaside resort of Scheveningen used to be a separate village, but over the years The Hague has spread out to meet it and it is now an extension of the main town. The main attractions are a long sandy beach, perfect for walking but often too windy and cold for bathing, and good fish restaurants. The **Kurhaus** (literally 'Cure House') is a striking Empire-style building, now housing a hotel, casino and several restaurants. The small resort of **Kijkduin**, 2 miles (3km) to the southwest, is quieter and more exclusive.

Accommodation

The Hague has some very fine hotels but they are not cheap. **Corona**, Buitenhof 39–42 (tel: (070) 363 7930). Four-star, 26 rooms; a small, friendly and very central hotel with antique-furnished rooms, impeccable service and a renowned French restaurant.

The pier at Scheveningen

Des Indes, Lange Voorhout 54–6 (tel: (070) 363 2932). Five-star, 80 rooms; palatial elegance, vast and beautifully furnished rooms. Famed as the former haunt of Mata Hari, who was executed in 1917 accused of being a spy.

Eating Out

The elegant restaurants of The Hague cater for the diplomatic community, and quality (as well as the prices) is very high.
Da Roberto, Noordeinde 196 (tel: (070) 346 4977). Highly original Italian dishes.
Radan Ajoe, Lange Poten 31 (tel: (070) 364 4592). Very smart, Indonesian, serving *rijsttafel*, rice with various spicy dishes.
Royal Dynasty, Noordeinde 123 (tel: (070) 365 2598). Superb oriental food, a blend of Cantonese, Thai and Indonesian.
Saur, Lange Vorhout 47–53 (tel: (070) 346 3344). French restaurant famed beyond the city for seafood, especially lobster and oysters, and its club-like atmosphere.

DORDRECHT

Dordrecht, known locally as
Dort, lies on one of the busiest
waterway junctions in Europe –
over 1,500 ships pass through
this junction every day. The
Beneden Merwede (a
continuation of the Rhine)
carries ships east towards
Germany, the Noord Merwede
heads north to Rotterdam while
the Dordtse Kil takes a slightly
different westerly route to
Rotterdam's Europoort. As a
result, Dordrecht's harbour –
the Nieuwe Haven – is often
crowded with a great variety of
ships and creaking barges,
moored two or three deep. The
harbour area also has some of
the town's best 17th and 18th-
century architecture, and many
of its former warehouses are
undergoing conversion to
apartments as part of an
ambitious urban renewal
scheme.

The Grote Kerk, Dordrecht

◆◆
DORDRECHTS MUSEUM
Museumstraat 40
This fine museum has a notable
collection of 17th century
paintings by artists born in
Dordrecht, including Aelbert
Cuyp, Nicolaes Maes, and
Rembrandt's pupil Ferdinand
Bol. It is definitely worth a visit if
you like Dutch landscape
painting, though the collection
also includes Impressionist-
style works. Good temporary
exhibitions are also held here
throughout the year.
Open: Tue–Sat 10.00–17.00hrs,
Sun 13.00–17.00hrs.

◆
GROTE KERK (Great Church)
Grotekerksplein
There was a chapel here in the
Middle Ages but the present
church, built in the style known
as Brabant Gothic, dates to the
late 15th century. It is worth
clambering up the 279 steps to
the top of the tower for an
excellent view over the town
and an opportunity to examine
the workings of the 49-bell
carillon.

◆
MUSEUM SIMON VAN GIJN
Niewe Haven 29
This lovely old house was built
in 1729 for the Burgomaster of
Dordrecht. It was subsequently
acquired by Simon van Gijn, a
highly successful banker, who
bequeathed the house and its
contents to the nation in 1922.
The fine rooms are beautifully
furnished in a variety of styles,
and the ground floor is devoted
to a delightful toy museum.
Open: Tue–Sat 10.00–17.00hrs,
Sun 13.00–17.00hrs.

GOUDA

Gouda is the archetypal Dutch town, with numerous canals bisecting the cobbled streets and a very pretty old centre. Visitors gain a real flavour of the Netherlands just by spending a few hours wandering about town. Although founded in the 13th century, Gouda's prosperity dates to the 17th century when the cheese trade developed. At the same time, English migrants introduced the manufacture of clay tobacco pipes which led to a flourishing pottery industry. The famous Gouda cheeses, protected by yellow wax, continue to be a predominant source of trade. On Thursday mornings in July and August they are sold at the colourful cheese and handicrafts market which fills the main square, Markt. The cheeses are loaded and unloaded by porters dressed in traditional costume. You will also find stalls selling locally made pottery and candles. Gouda also specialises in syrup-filled waffles, known as *Goudse*, which are sold from open stalls in the town.

♦♦
HET CATHARINA GASTHUIS
Oosthaven 9–10
The Hospice of St Catherine was founded as an almshouse for pilgrims and travellers in 1310, but the current building dates largely to 1665 when half was used as a hospital and the rest as the governor's house. It now contains an intriguing museum with a very good collection of paintings and several rooms furnished in

period style. The old infirmary can be visited as well as an 18th-century dispensary, where the surgical instruments displayed, including a tooth extractor, look more like tools of torture.
Open: Mon–Sat 10.00–17.00hrs, Sun 12.00–17.00hrs.

♦♦♦
SINT JANSKERK
Achter de Kerk 15–16
This huge Gothic church, dedicated to St John, is one of the most important in the Netherlands. It was rebuilt after a fire in 1552, and the 405 feet (123m) high nave is lit by an outstanding series of stained glass windows depicting scenes from the Bible and Dutch history. The 70 windows were given by a wide range of donors, including Philip II of Spain and William of Orange. Each chose themes relevant to their interests: William of Orange, for example, who was shortly to lead the Dutch revolt against Spanish rule, chose 'Christ Driving the Money Lenders from the Temple'. It is worth buying the guide on sale at the door to understand what each window is portraying.

♦
STADHUIS (Town Hall)
Markt
In the centre of the main square, this wonderful Gothic building of the mid 15th century is impossible to miss. Note the highly decorated façade, with its flamboyant statues of the Burgundian dukes and duchesses who ruled the region until their title passed to the Habsburgs in 1482.

Excursions from Gouda

An exceptionally pretty and rewarding drive links Gouda to Utrecht. From Gouda take the road through **Oudewater** (stop here to look at the witches' scales in the Heksenwaag in the town centre), **Montfoort** and **Linschoten**, rejoining the motorway for the last stretch. The landscape is typically Dutch and the villages are simple and attractive.

A little way northeast of Gouda, the **Reeuwijkse Plassen** (lakes) are a magnet for water sports enthusiasts and are worth visiting as an area of natural beauty in their own right.

Gouda's Sint Janskerk

LEIDEN (LEYDEN)

The life of Leiden revolves around the university, the oldest in the country. William the Silent bestowed the first university charter in 1575 to reward the courageous townsfolk who had withstood a Spanish siege lasting 131 days. Leiden is very proud of its cultural connections and of the fact that Rembrandt was born in the town in 1606. The town has many fine buildings and museums grouped around the banks of the Rijn (Rhine) and the university quarter, which stretches either side of Rapenburg. This quarter bustles with students and bicycles in term-time, and the numerous cheap and cheerful cafés cater for a moderate purse; the atmosphere is refreshing, especially if you have just come from one of the hotter tourist spots.

◆

MOLENMUSEUM DE VALK

2E Binnenvestgracht 1

This stately windmill, dating to 1743, is incongruously situated in the middle of a car park but is worth visiting for the views from the seventh floor. The other floors are used for informative displays on different kinds of windmills and their functions.

Open: Tue–Sat 10.00–17.00hrs, Sun 13.00–17.00hrs.

◆◆◆

RIJKSMUSEUM VAN OUHDHEDEN

Rapenburg 28

One of the main attractions of this museum is the collection of

ancient Egyptian mummies and other objects connected with the cult of the dead. Particularly chilling specimens include the mummy of a cat and that of a five-year-old child.
Classical antiquities from Greece and Rome are also a strong feature and a section is devoted to the archaeology of the Netherlands.
Open: Mon–Sat 10.00–17.00hrs, Sun 12.00–17.00hrs.

◆◆
RIJKSMUSEUM VOOR VOLKENKUNDE (National Museum of Ethnology)
Steenstraat 1
This huge collection consists of pieces from all over the world. There is a strong emphasis on material from the former Dutch colony of Indonesia – gorgeous masks, puppets and costumes – and from China and Japan.
Open: Tue–Sat 10.00–17.00hrs, Sun 13.00–17.00hrs.

◆
STEDELIJK MUSEUM DE LAKENHAL
Oude Singel 28–32
Lakenhal translates as 'Cloth Hall' and the building, dating from 1640, was once the

Leiden's Ethnology Museum

headquarters of the Cloth Makers Guild – hence the plaques on the façade illustrating spinning, weaving and dyeing. The museum gives the visitor further insights into this important industry and a good idea of the history of the town. Various rooms illustrate the work of surgeons, tailors, cloth-makers and brewers. There is also a traditional 18th-century kitchen and even an old Catholic church. The rooms at the rear are given over to a collection of paintings by Lieden-born artists, including Lucas van Leyden and an early Rembrandt.
Open: Tue–Sat 10.00–17.00hrs, Sun 13.00–17.00hrs.

Excursions from Leiden
A scenic route from Lieden to Rotterdam takes you through **Alphen aan de Rijn**, where you will find the Avifauna, a superb collection of exotic birds. Continue south beside the Gouwe canal and through Hillegersberg to Rotterdam for a pleasant trip and a change from the motorway.

ROTTERDAM

Rotterdam is the second biggest city in the Netherlands, after Amsterdam, but its appearance is entirely different to that of any other Dutch town. German bombs rained down on Rotterdam on 4 May 1940, destroying almost the whole of the old city. It has since rebuilt itself into a dynamic, modern city with the largest port in the world. Sitting at the mouth of the Nieuwe Maas river, the port is strategically positioned to receive huge ocean-going container ships and oil tankers. Inland barges then carry cargo along the Maas to the Rhine and its tributaries, penetrating deep into the heart of mainland Europe.

The centre of Rotterdam has all the shops and sophistication you would expect of a major city, though the pedestrian malls, office blocks and cultural centres are modern and functional rather than beautiful. Examples of experimental architecture are dotted

throughout the city but the most intriguing are located in the Oudehaven area. Here you will find Piet Blom's striking **Kijk-Kubus** (Cube Houses), an animated shopping mall and bustling waterside cafés. By complete contrast, the area around Delfshaven escaped bombing and its 17th-century buildings give some idea of how Rotterdam used to be. As its name implies, Delfshaven once belonged to Delft, when Rotterdam was a mere village and Delft an important city. Only in 1886 was Delfshaven finally incorporated into Rotterdam. Delfshaven witnessed an important event in 1620 when the Pilgrim Fathers (Puritan refugees from England) set sail from here, bound for America, on board *The Speedwell.* This ship proved unseaworthy and the pilgrims were towed to dock at Plymouth, in England, before continuing their historic voyage in *The Mayflower.*

The modern Europoort complex lies to the west of the city and it can be seen by taking a boat trip or by

Boymans-Van Beuningen Museum

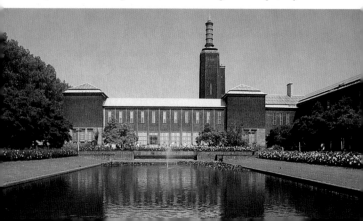

following the well-marked
'Rotterdamse Havenroute' by
car. The total length of this tour
– 50 miles (80km) – gives some
indication of the vast size of the
port and the huge volume of
shipping that passes through it.
Details of boat tours
(*Havenrondvaarten*) are
available from the tourist office.

◆◆◆
BOYMANS-VAN BEUNINGEN MUSEUM
Mathenesserlaan 18–20
This is a large and exciting
museum. Its collections cover
paintings from the 14th century
to the present day, sculpture,
ceramics – including Delftware
– silver, lace, old clocks and
many other items. Brueghel,
Rembrandt, Rubens and Bosch
are only some of the well-
known painters represented.
The modern section is
considered to be one of the
best in Europe and includes
important Surrealist works by
Dali, Ernst and Magritte.
Open: Tue–Sat 10.00–17.00hrs,
Sun 11.00–17.00hrs.

◆
EUROMAST
Parkhaven 20
If the weather is good this is the
perfect place to start a tour of
Rotterdam. The views from the
320 feet (100m) Euromast
stretch over the whole of the
city and to the Europoort,
where you can watch the
comings and goings of
hundreds of ships. The
Euromast was completed in
1960 for the Floriade flower
festival. The **Space Tower**,
which now sits on top, was
added more recently, adding

another 280 feet (85m) to the
height. Visitors with a good
head for heights can ascend to
the Space Cabin at the top for
even more panoramic views.

◆◆
MARITIEM MUSEUM PRINS HENDRIK
Leauvehaven 1
Rotterdam's Maritime Museum
is split into indoor and outdoor
sections. Inside there is a
collection of model ships, both
ancient and modern, examples
of the several types of barge
that can be seen on the canals
of the Netherlands, and various
maps and nautical instruments.
The outdoor part is rather more
fun, with a selection of real
boats dating from the 19th
century. The *pièce de résistance*
is the warship *De Buffel*, built in
1868. Visitors can see the
sleeping, eating and bathing
arrangements of the officers
and crew, the captain's
luxurious quarters and all the
workings of this beautifully
restored and polished ship.
Open: Tue–Sat 10.00–17.00hrs,
Sun 11.00–17.00hrs.

Maritiem Museum Prins Hendrik

Excursions from Rotterdam

The **Molens van Kinderdijk** (Kinderdijk Windmills) lie 10 miles (16km) east of Rotterdam on the River Lek, just north of Alblasserdam. These 19 windmills were once used to drain excess water from the Alblasserwaard polders into the Lek. This task is now performed by electrical pumps and today the windmills only operate for the benefit of tourists. The Kinderdijk mill complex provides a useful introduction to the different types of mill that

The Euromast, Rotterdam

you will see as you travel around the Netherlands. *Open*: Apr–Sep, Mon–Sat 09.30–17.30hrs. The mills work on Saturdays during July and August, and they are illuminated at night during the first week in September.

Accommodation

Rotterdam has a good range of hotels, although some of the nearby towns offer rather prettier options.

Emma, Nieuwe Binnenweg 6 (tel: (010) 436 5533). Three-star, 24 rooms; functional but good value bed and breakfast establishment close to the Boymans-van Beuningen Museum.

Rotterdam Hilton, Weena 10 (tel: (010) 414 4044). Five-star, 252 rooms; reliable comfort in the centre of town – expensive.

Parkhotel, Westersingel 70 (tel: (010) 436 3611). Four-star, 199 rooms; a characterful hotel with art deco flourishes, gardens and fitness centre.

Eating Out

Le Coq d'Or, Van Vollenhoven-straat 25 (tel: (010) 436 0242). Michelin-star quality and prices, superb *menu gastronomique*, and garden for summer dining.

Dewi Sri, Westerkade 2022 (tel: (010) 436 0263). The interior is reminiscent of a colonial club, with a choice of four different Indonesian banquets (*rijsttafels*), each one a feast of colours, textures and flavours.

Old Dutch Rochussenstraat 20 (tel: (010) 436 0242). Rustic-style beamed house serving traditional Dutch food plus lighter fish and vegetarian dishes.

ZEELAND

Zeeland province consists of a series of islands and peninsulas linked by dams and bridges. Zeeland, perhaps more than any other part of the Netherlands, has always been in the forefront of the constant battle with the sea. Land and towns that have taken centuries to build up have sometimes been destroyed by violent floods and storms in a matter of a few hours. The most recent serious flood occurred in 1953 when nearly 2,000 people were killed and 100,000 were left homeless. This prompted demands for a flood-protection system that would prevent such a disaster from ever happening again. As a result the Delta Plan was born, involving the construction of a massive tidal barrier that now protects much of Zeeland's vulnerable coastline.

The story of the Delta Plan is told at the Delta Expo (see right). This makes a good starting point for understanding the delicate relationship that the Netherlands has with the sea. Aside from the engineering achievement, the Delta Plan has turned Zeeland province into a paradise for visitors who enjoy water sports. Zeeland is also renowned for its bathing beaches, its bird life and fishing, and for restaurants serving top quality seafood. Visitors to the southernmost point of the province, Zeeland Flanders, can rarely resist the chance to visit Ghent or Antwerp in neighbouring Belgium.

◆◆◆
THE DELTA EXPO ✓

Neeltje Jans island – nearest town, Burg-Haamstede
This fascinating exhibition is housed in a service building set on an artificial island in the middle of the Oosterschelde (Eastern Scheldt) estuary. To reach the island you drive across the top of the Oosterschelderkering, a huge tidal barrier completed in 1986. The Delta Expo complex has a comprehensive collection of exhibits, including scale models and multi-lingual audio-visual presentations, explaining the history and development of the Delta Plan. After the floods of 1953, the Delta Act of 1958 laid out plans for a series of conventional dams that would protect the region from further disaster. The dams at Veersgat, Haringvliet and Brouwershaven were completed by 1972. The projects ran into strong opposition, however, when work began on the final phase, which would have closed off the Oosterschelde estuary from the North Sea and brought an end to the valuable oyster, mussel and lobster trade. Environmentalists and fishermen joined forces to warn of the loss of valuable fishing waters and an ecologically rich environment. After much intensive study it was decided that the desired safety levels could be achieved without completely sealing off the estuary. The solution was to construct a storm-surge barrier at the mouth of the Oosterschelde, consisting of

Bascule bridge, Middelburg

huge moveable steel gates.
These are closed during
periods of exceptionally high
tides or potentially damaging
storms, but are left open at
other times so that the normal
tidal flow is not interrupted. The
mudflats and saltmarshes of the
Zeeland delta have thus been
preserved, to the benefit of
fishermen and wildlife alike.
The development of this huge
feat of engineering, and the
workings of both the barrier
and the dams, are explained by
excellent models showing the
effects of the tides on the
surrounding landscape. At the
end of the tour visitors are
taken down to visit a section of
the barrier; here you can
appreciate the scale of the
works and the force of the
water.
Open: Apr–Oct, daily
10.00–17.00hrs; Nov–Mar,
Wed–Sun 10.00–17.00hrs.

◆
GOES
Heading south from the Delta
Expo you can drive along dam-
top roads to visit the islands of
Beveland and Walcheren.
Goes, located on South
Beveland, is one of Zeeland's
largest towns, its elegant centre
surrounded by 15th-century
ramparts. The 18th-century
rococo façade added to the
town hall on **Grote Markt** (the
main square) is a notable
feature. The town also has a
small local history museum, the
Museum van Noord en Zuid
Beveland. Luxury yachts mingle
with traditional sailing barges in
the attractive harbour. It is well
worth taking a trip on the
Stooomtram (South Beveland
Steam Railway) which chugs in
summer from Goes to
Oudelande through typical
Zeeland scenery of lakes,
woods and dykes.

MIDDELBURG

The capital of Zeeland
province, Middelburg suffered
heavy bombing during World
War II, but the historic buildings
of the compact city centre have
been well restored. Beautiful
old buildings surround **Markt**,
the main square and the venue
for an important market held
every Thursday. Stallholders
dress in traditional local
costumes for the day, and
antiques are a speciality. The
Markt is surrounded by
restaurants and cafés, from
where you can watch all the
goings on. The surrounding
side streets also contain some
fascinating antique shops.

◆◆

ABDIJKERKEN
(Abbey Churches)
Onderdentoren

This unusual complex consists of three churches, originally dating to the 9th century. Following the Dutch revolt against Spanish rule, the monks were ejected and, from 1574, the monastery was converted to form the seat of provincial government. The three churches, the States Hall and the Zeeuws Museum (Zeeland Museum), located in the cloister, can all be visited. You can also climb Lange Jan (Long John), the 300 foot (91m) tower. The abbey's carillon is one of Zeeland's most memorable; carillon concerts are given once a week throughout the year and twice a week in summer.

The Stadhuis, Middelburg

◆

STADHUIS (Town Hall)
Markt

Overlooking Markt, the main square, this is a remarkable building. The 15th-century façade dominates the square and has 25 statues of the Counts and Countesses of Zeeland set between the Gothic windows. The building received a severe battering during World War II but has been well restored. The pinnacled tower and former Vleeshall (Meat Market), now used for exhibitions, were added in the 16th century.

Accommodation

Most of Middelburg's hotels are located in the area around Markt or around the station (only a 10-minute walk away). **Wapen van Middelburg**, Pottenmarkt 12-20 (tel: (01180) 14706); a friendly and very central hotel.

VEERE

Veere lies 5 miles (8km) north
of Middelburg and is one of the
most delightful little towns in the
Netherlands. Between the 14th
and 18th centuries, Veere
prospered as the main Dutch
port for Scottish wool imports.
Today the Scottish connection
remains only in the twinning of
Culross with Veere. The town
also traded in linen and salt and
was important enough for the
East India Company to set up
an office for handling imports
from the Far East. Construction
of the Delta Plan barrier
brought an end to Veere's role
as a major port, and its
economy is now restricted to
tourism and leisure boating. It
has a very attractive main
square – a leafy area of grass
and trees encircled by
cobbled streets. The square
also has unusual brick houses
with step gables and distinctive
shutter decorations: some are
painted dark green and white,
others red and black. Some of
the best cafés are to be found
around the harbour, which is
lined with yachts and old sailing
barges.

Oude Stadhuis, Veere

◆
GROTE KERK (Great Church)
Oudestraat
This massive church dates to
the 14th century but time has
taken its toll. Napoleonic troops
used it as a barracks and
destroyed the stained glass,
leaving only its original shell,
now used for exhibitions and
cultural programmes. Good
views over the town are to be
had by climbing the tower. The
16th-century Gothic town well
by the church is worth seeing.

◆◆
OUDE STADHUIS
(Old Town Hall)
Markt 5
The façade of this unusual two-
storey Gothic building is
decorated with statues of the
lords and ladies of Veere. A 48-
bell carillon hangs inside an
onion-shaped belfry. The
building itself houses the town's
museum, in which a silver
goblet given to Maximillan of
Buren by the Holy Roman
Emperor, Charles V, has pride
of place.

◆
SCHOTZE HUIZEN
(Scottish Houses)
Kaai 25 and 27
These 16th-century Gothic-style
houses stand next to each other
on the quay. No 25, built in
1539, is called Het Lammetje
('The Lamb'); the figure of a
lamb, symbol of the wool trade,
is engraved into its stone
façade. No 27, built in 1561, is
enigmatically called De Struys
('The Ostrich'). Both houses
were used as warehouses and
offices by Scottish wool
merchants who lived in Veere.

Lifting bridge, Zierikzee

Today they house a museum giving details of the local fishing industry and decorated with old books, period furniture and traditional Zeeland costumes. *Open*: Apr–Oct, Mon 13.00–17.00hrs, Tue–Sat 10.00–17.00hrs.

Accommodation

Veere's hotels are simple, but this is a charming town in which to stay.

De Campveerse Toren, Kade 2 (tel: (01181) 1291). Two star, 16 rooms; located on the quay, with most rooms giving a view of the sea, and a good restaurant. Reputed to be the oldest inn in the Netherlands.

't Waepen van Veere, Markt 23-7 (tel: 01181) 1231). Two star, 14 rooms; overlooking the pretty main square. Simple accommodation and a large, busy restaurant.

Eating Out

D'Ouwe Werf, Bastion 2 (tel: (01181) 1493). Well-recommended restaurant in a splendid house, with a commanding position above the harbour.

Excursions from Veere

Only a few miles west of Veere is a lovely stretch of coast where **Oostkapelle** and **Domburg** (the oldest bathing resort in Zeeland) offer lots of seaside facilities and excellent beaches.

ZIERIKZEE

Zierikzee is located on the island of Schouwen–Duiveland and is the largest and most important town in this part of Zeeland. The location of the town, on the Oosterschelde estuary and a tributary of the Gouwe, enabled it to become an important port between the 14th and 16th centuries, trading salt with England, Flanders (now part of Belgium) and the rest of the Netherlands. Another local product was madder, a coastal plant whose dried roots were highly valued as a source of crimson dye. The harbour expanded to meet demand and is now filled with yachts in summer. The mixture of medieval fortifications and elegant 17th-century merchants' houses, located along the canals and around the old harbour, give the visitor much to admire. On Thursday the town fills up for the weekly market held in the main square. In summer there is an additional market on Tuesdays.

◆

'S GRAVENSTEEN
Mol 25
This 16th-century building, with its crow-stepped gable, was a prison until 1923 and now houses a maritime museum. Visitors can peer into the prisoners' dormitories, and read their graffiti. The museum is full of model ships, maps and all things related to Zierikzee's constant battle against the sea.
Open: May–Sep, Mon–Sat 10.00–17.00hrs, Sun 12.00–17.00hrs.

◆

NOBELPORT (Nobel Gate)

This gate in the city walls is flanked by two round towers with pepperpot roofs. Dating to the 14th century, it is the oldest surviving part of Zierikzee's fortifications.

◆

OUDE HAVEN (Old Harbour)
This characterful part of the town has many fine 17th to19th-century buildings. Each end of Oude Haven is defended by ancient water-gates: Noordhavenpoort (North Port Gate) is a fine double-gated building dating to 1559 and contrasts with the 15th-century Zuidhavenport (South Port Gate), a square tower with four corner turrets.

STADHUIS (Town Hall)
Meelstraat 6–8
Zierikzee's town hall has a particularly attractive 14th-century octagonal wooden tower, formerly used as a meat market. The museum inside gives further insights into the town's history and contains some gruesome instruments of torture.
Open: May–Nov, Mon–Fri 11.00–17.00hrs.

◆

WINDMILLS
Zierikzee has two surviving windmills, built to grind corn. De Hoop, built in 1874, is at Lang Nobelstraat 43, and Den Haas, built in 1727, is on Bolwerk.
Open: Sat 09.00–16.00hrs.

Accommodation
Zierikzee has a couple of moderate hotels in the centre of the town.
Mondragon, Havenpark 21 (tel: (01110) 13051). Three-star, 9 rooms; overlooking the canal and close to the main square. There is a good restaurant in a separate building a few doors away.
Monique, Driekoningenin 7 (tel: (01110) 12323). With 16 rooms the hotel is inexpensive, but there are no TVs in the bedrooms.

Eating Out
Concordia, Applemarkt 29 (tel: (01110) 15122) serves typical Dutch dishes.
t' Zeeuwsche Pannekoekenhuis, Applemarkt 6 (tel: (01110) 16179) – delicious pancakes.

UTRECHT

The province of Utrecht lies at the heart of the Netherlands and is easily reached by road or rail. This is also the smallest province, with no substantial towns apart from the city of Utrecht itself. The city came into existence as a Christian bishopric founded by St Wilibrord around AD700. Subsequent Bishops of Utrecht expanded their influence well beyond the confines of the city, and they were once a powerful political force in the Netherlands.

The city itself is compact with an old centre bordered by the main canals. Parking is available underneath the vast modern Hoog Catharijne shopping centre at the west end of the town. This is also the first building that railway travellers

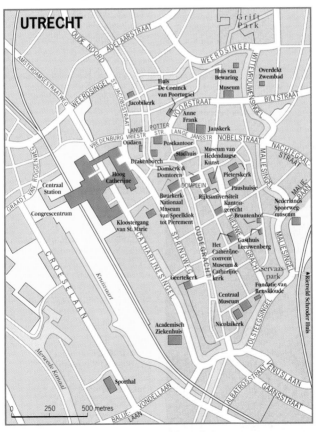

will see, since the shopping centre lies between the station and the town centre. Leaving the Hoog Catharijne complex, simply head in the direction of the unmissable Domtoren, the cathedral tower. The first sound you are likely to hear is the carillon of the Dom – a sound that echoes beautifully off the closely packed houses along the canals.

You will soon encounter the **Oudegracht** (Old Canal) which threads right through the heart of the city, providing a natural focus for shops, cafés and street markets. The cafés of Oudegracht are often full of students, whose presence lends a lively atmosphere to the town.

View from Utrecht's Domtoren

The university here was established in 1636 and is now the largest in the Netherlands. The main campus is to the east of the town but the centre is full of older university buildings, some of which can be visited.

CENTRAAL MUSEUM (Central Museum)
Agnietenstraat 1

The main attraction here is the collection of 16th and 17th-century paintings by local artists, notably Jan van Scorel, who brought Italian influence into the Utrecht School of painting, and his pupils, such as Maerten van Heemskerck and Antoon Mor. There is a fine collection of modern Dutch paintings, and an assortment of objects related to the history and archaeology of the region. *Open*: Tue–Sat 10.00–17.00hrs, Sun 13.00–17.00hrs.

DOMKERK (Cathedral)
Domplein

There is little left of the main body of the cathedral which collapsed in a hurricane which hit the town in 1674. The Gothic choir and transepts remain, and some of the 15th-century wall paintings. The peaceful 14th-century cloisters linking the cathedral with the university buildings are worth a visit.

DOMTOREN (Cathedral Tower)
Domplein

This superb Gothic tower took more than 250 years to complete – from 1254 to 1517. At 367 feet (112m) it is the tallest church tower in the Netherlands. If you can make it to the top you are rewarded with excellent views over the town and the surrounding countryside.

◆◆◆

NATIONAL MUSEUM VAN SPEELKLOK TOT PIEREMENT (National Museum from Musical Clock to the Barrel Organ)
Buurkerkhof 10
As its name spells out, this entrancing museum covers the history of mechanical musical instruments, from large and colourful street organs to honky-tonk pianolas and orchestrinas. Visitors join a jolly tour each hour which includes a demonstration of many of the instruments and an explanation of their workings. Street organs are still a common sight in Utrecht and all over the Netherlands, particularly on market days.
Open: Tue–Sat 10.00–17.00hrs, Sun 13.00–17.00hrs.

◆

NEDERLANDS SPOORWEGMUSEUM (Dutch Railway Museum)
Maliebaanstation
Housed in the disused 19th-century Maliebaan railway station, this museum covers the history of the Dutch railways, from the earliest days of steam to the age of the TGV, by means of working models, films and paintings. The covered trackways outside are used for static displays of steam engines, trams and carriages.
Open: Tue–Sat 10.00–17.00hrs, Sun 13.00–17.00hrs.

◆◆◆
RIETVELD-SCHRODERHUIS ✓

Prins Hendriklaan 50A
This imaginative modern house was designed by Gerrit Rietveld (1888–1964), a leading member of the Dutch de Stijl architectural movement, along with his client Truus Schroder. The radical design is all the more startling by contrast with its neighbours, a row of unexceptional 19th-century houses. Truus Schroder had well defined requirements: she wanted every room to have an external door and plenty of natural light, and she wanted the whole to be as economical in space and energy as possible. The upper floor, in which she spent most of her time, has sliding doors so that it can be turned into one large open-plan room or divided up when required. Guest bedrooms were located below, and Gerrit Rietveld himself lived here for some time. The design is ingenious and the house should not be missed.

The Rietveld-Schroderhuis

◆◆
RIJKSMUSEUM HET CATHARIJNECONVENT
Nieuwegracht 63
This 16th-century Carmelite convent now houses a superb museum of ecclesiastical and religious art illustrating both the Catholic and Protestant traditions in the Netherlands. The collection includes vestments, altarpieces and sculpture. There are also some fascinating manuscripts, and one floor is devoted to the history of religious development in Utrecht.
Open: Tue–Fri 10.00–17.00hrs, Sat–Sun 11.00–17.00hrs.

Accommodation
The choice here is rather limited and most of the reasonable hotels are on the outskirts of town.
Des Pays Bas, Janskerkhof 10 (tel: (030) 333321). Four-star, 47 rooms; an old-fashioned place with a lived-in feel. Bedrooms are adequate with small bathrooms, but the position is very central.
Holiday Inn, Jaarbeursplein 24 (tel: (030) 910555). Four-star, 280 rooms; all that you would expect from a Holiday Inn, well equipped if functional, and in a reasonably central position close to the station.

Brown café conviviality

Mitland, Ariënslaan 1 (tel: (030) 715824). Three-star, 44 rooms; in an attractive parkland setting northeast of the centre; you will need a car, but this is a modern, comfortable and reasonably priced hotel.

Eating Out
There are hundreds of restaurants and cafés all over the town, some catering for the student purse, others more sophisticated. The **Oudegracht** is the best place to find both bars and restaurants.

Shopping
The **Hoog Catharijne** complex, by the railway station, is the largest covered shopping centre in the Netherlands. For a very different kind of shopping experience go in search of one of the many street markets in Utrecht – there is some kind of market going on every day of the week and the VVV tourist office will supply the details.

Excursions from Utrecht
To the northwest of Utrecht take the A27 towards Hilversum and head for the **Loosdrechtse Plassen** (lakes). The numerous small lakes, created by peat extractions, cover an area of 6,250 acres (2,500ha). Pretty lake villages, such as **Loenen** and **Breukelen**, add to the region's picturesque appeal. Water sports are very popular in this area but have not spoiled the general atmosphere of calm and peacefulness. For the less energetic there are a number of castles that can be visited, including **Kasteel Sypesteyn** at Nieuw Loosdrecht, and Slot Zuylen at Oud-Zuilen.

NOORD BRABANT

Noord (North) Brabant is the Netherland's largest province, and it shares a long border with Belgium to the south. The province is economically important because of its coal mines and the industrial towns of Eindhoven, Helmond and Tilburg. More appealing to the visitor are the historic cities of Breda and 's Hertogenbosch (Den Bosch), and the extensive wood and fenland recreational reserves of the Biesbos.

BREDA

Breda was granted its city charter in 1252 and the town had a succession of feudal rulers over the next 250 years, as the lordship was either sold or passed on through marriage alliances.

It was Hendrik III, of the Dutch house of Nassau, who in 1504 built the town's castle and extensive fortifications. He married Princess Claudia of the French house of Orange. Their son, Réné, became the first Prince of Orange–Nassau. Réné was succeeded in 1544 by William the Silent, who spent much of his life in Breda and led the Dutch Revolt against Spanish rule.

Breda was at the forefront of the revolt, and despite its fortifications it was ransacked by the Spanish in 1581. It remained in Spanish hands for nine years, during which William the Silent was assassinated in Delft. His successor, Prince Maurice of Nassau, retook Breda in 1590 by hiding his troops in a cargo

Grote Kerk, Breda

of peat destined to supply the Spanish garrison with fuel. The peat barge was admitted into Breda's citadel, where the Dutch soldiers routed the Spanish.

The town subsequently surrendered to the Spanish again in 1625 after a nine-month siege, and it was not until 1637 that Prince Frederick Henry finally ejected the Spanish for good.

England's King Charles II lived in Breda during his exile, and it was from here that he issued his Declaration of Breda in 1660, outlining his terms for returning to England and accepting the throne.

Today Breda is the most attractive town in Noord Brabant and makes an excellent base for exploring the area. The atmosphere is relaxed and the centre of the town has some lovely old buildings, good shops and restaurants.

BEGIJNHOF
Catharinastraat
This peaceful and charming group of 16th-century houses was built as a convent for the lay order of Begijns (Begines), women who devoted their lives to religion and charitable works but without taking vows of chastity, poverty and obedience. It is now occupied by elderly women of upstanding character, who tend the small herb garden and look after the Catholic chapel.

◆◆
GROTE KERK
Grote Markt
The original church on this site was founded in the 13th century. In its present form the church is largely the result of 15th-century rebuilding. The style is predominantly Gothic, with a touch of baroque in the onion-shaped dome on the tower. The church is notable for its outstanding tombs and monuments, in which you can trace the complex lineage of the Counts of Breda, Nassau and Orange-Nassau. The most striking memorial is the Renaissance tomb of Count Engelbrecht II of Nassau, Captain General of the Netherlands, who died of consumption in 1504. The huge alabaster monument was carved by Italian masons, and is supported by corner figures representing Caesar, Hannibal, Regulus and Philip of Macedonia. By contrast, the misericords in the choir present a sequence of satirical carvings – they were carved over

several centuries, some as recently as 1954. The finely decorated organ, which dates in part to the 16th century, is regularly used for concerts in the peak season.

◆
KASTEEL
Kasteelplein
Breda's citadel is now a military academy and can only be visited through occasional tours. Even so, you can view the exterior from the attractive **Valkenburg** park which surrounds the Kasteel. A castle stood on this site as early as 1198, and the present building was commissioned in 1536 by Hendrik III, whose statue stands in Kasteelplein. **Spanjaardsgat** (Spaniard's Gate), on nearby Kraanstraat, is a twin-towered water-gate, popularly said to be the point at which Prince Maurice smuggled his troops into the Spanish Garrison.

◆◆

RIJKSMUSEUM VOOR VOLKENKUNDE
(Ethnographic Museum)
Kasteelplein 25
This interesting museum has exhibits from all over the world, with a strong emphasis on Indonesian culture.
Open: Tue–Sat 10.00–17.00hrs, Sun 13.00–17.00hrs.

◆◆

STEDELIJK EN BISSCHOPPELIJK (Municipal and Episcopal Museum)
Grote Markt
This museum is housed in a fine 17th-century building, and, as the name implies, covers the secular and ecclesiastical

history of Breda. The displays include a large collection of religious paintings and ecclesiastical oddments, including some finely embroidered vestments. *Open*: Wed–Sat 10.30–17.00hrs, Tue, Sun 13.00–17.00hrs.

Excursions from Breda

Around 10 miles (16km) northwest of Breda, off the A27, is the **Biesbos** (Reed Wood), one of the largest nature reserves in the Netherlands. The Biesbos was created in the 15th century, when the sea defences of Zuid (South) Holland gave way, flooding a vast expanse of land and destroying some 70 towns and villages. The sea defences were never repaired so that, in time, the Biesbos developed into a huge area of reed beds, supporting a plethora of sea and bird life (see **Peace and Quiet**).

Saturday market in Den Bosch

'S HERTOGENBOSCH

Also known as Den Bosch, the name, which means Duke's Wood, dates from the 12th century when Henry I, Duke of Brabant, built a hunting lodge here. Today, the main draw for visitors is the cathedral, one of the best Gothic churches in the Netherlands. Den Bosch was also the birthplace of the renowned artist Hieronymus Bosch (1450–1516), an extraordinary painter whose strange and sometimes frightening pictures stay in the mind. Sadly, the city has none of his great works – these are now in the Boymans-Van Beuningen Museum in Rotterdam or in the Prado in Madrid, taken by Philip II of Spain during the Spanish occupation of the Netherlands.

◆
MARKT

The centre of the city, this is the site of the Wednesday and Saturday markets. A commemorative bronze statue of Hieronymus Bosch stands proudly in front of the 16th-century Stadhuis (Town Hall), which was given a new classical façade in 1671. The carillon, complete with mechanical horsemen, chimes every half hour. On Wednesdays there is an hour-long bell recital, beginning at 10.00hrs.

◆◆
NOORDBRABANTS MUSEUM
Verwersstraat 41
This is an excellent example of an interesting and informative regional museum. Housed in the 18th-century mansion of the

former provincial governor, the collection includes archaeological finds, drawings by Hieronymus Bosch, Van Gogh's *Study of a Brabant Peasant* and details of popular local traditions and historical events.

Open: Tue–Fri 10.00–17.00hrs, Sat 11.00–17.00hrs.

◆◆◆
ST JANSKATHEDRAAL
(St John's Cathedral)
Parade

Built between 1330 and 1530, this is considered to be the finest Gothic cathedral in the Netherlands. Restoration over the years has only accentuated the beauty of the interior. Your eyes are drawn, as you enter, to the soaring vault delicately painted with floral motifs, and the huge traceried windows. Look out for the exquisitely carved 15th-century pews, the much-revered figure of the Madonna in the Lady Chapel to which many miracles have been attributed, and the Altar of the Passion, painted in 1500, in St Anthony's Chapel. The carillon plays on Wednesdays from 12.00–13.00hrs.

St Janskathedraal, Den Bosch

◆
SLAGER MUSEUM
Choorstraat 16

This museum is dedicated to the paintings of three generations of the Slager family who, between them, have been producing portraits and pictures of Den Bosch for more than 130 years. Petrus Slager (1841–1912) was the first to wield a paint brush, and the present generation is represented by Tom Slager, born in 1918, who now lives in France.

Open: Tue–Fri, Sun 14.00–17.00hrs.

Excursions from 's Hertogenbosch

Around 15 miles (24km) west of Den Bosch, at Kaatsheuvel, is **Efteling**, a family theme park with thrill and fantasy rides based on traditional tales and legends (*open*: mid Apr–late Oct, daily 10.00–18.00hrs; also Aug, Mon 19.30hrs to midnight).

At Rosmalen, 4 miles (6km) northeast, the **Autotron** (Automobile Museum) is a must for the car buff. Here you can trace the development of some of the world's most famous cars, and some of the most obscure. This is one of the largest car museums in Europe, and you can see restoration of yet more models in progress. At Waalwijk, about 5 miles (8km) west of Den Bosch, there is the **Nederlands Leder en Schoenenmuseum** (Dutch Leather and Shoe Museum).The collection includes shoes from all over the world, as well as a 19th-century tannery.

LIMBURG

Limburg, the southernmost province of the Netherlands, is something of an oddity compared to the rest of the country. It is, for example, relatively hilly, especially around Maastricht where the province is sandwiched between Germany to the east and Belgium to the south and west. Limburg also has a distinctly Catholic culture, which it shares with the neighbouring Dutch province of Noord Brabant. Both provinces were allowed to remain Catholic after the Dutch Revolt of the 1570s when the rest of the Netherlands turned Protestant. This culture is most evident in the flamboyant church architecture and in the region's colourful carnival celebrations which take place in the three days before Ash Wednesday.

The people of Limburg have a strong affinity with their neighbours in the Belgian province of the same name, and they even speak Dutch with a softer accent, more akin to Flemish. They are a cosmopolitan people, and receptive to other influences – hardly surprising when you consider that few points in Limburg are ever more than 8 miles (13km) from the German and Belgian borders. The people of Maastricht, in particular, see themselves as belonging to a model European city of the future, where three languages, three currencies and three diverse cuisines all contribute to the rich mix.

HEERLEN

Heerlen has been described as an overgrown shopping centre with nothing much to delay the tourist. It does, however, have a rich past, and it would be a pity to pass by without seeing the excellent Thermenmuseum built around the Roman baths.

◆◆
THERMENMUSEUM
Coriovallum Straat 9
Heerlen started out as *Coriovallum*, an important Roman trading town on the road built to link Köln (Cologne) and Calais. The extensive remains of the Roman baths, along with several shops, were excavated in the 1960s and are now preserved within a modern hanger-like structure. Visitors look down from a steel walkway over the excavated baths, and taped commentaries explain the various parts of the complex. Other finds, including pottery, coins, jewellery and statues are also displayed, and the whole site is explained by films and other documentation.
Open: Tue–Fri 10.00–17.00hrs.

The metalworkers' art

MAASTRICHT

Maastricht is the capital of Limburg province and is one of the most exciting cities in the Netherlands. It is also one of the country's oldest cities, having been founded by the Romans as *Mosae Trajectum*, meaning 'the crossing over the River Maas'. At various times the city has been taken over by the French, the Spanish and most recently, during World War II, by the Germans. Despite past troubles, Maastricht today revels in its internationalism, and as soon as you arrive in the city you feel as though you were in a different country. It was no surprise that Maastricht was chosen for the important 1991 European summit at which the member nations of the European Community debated a number of measures that would bind them closer together. Maastricht is, in many respects, already a unified Europe in miniature – its shops, cafés and restaurants accept Dutch, German and Belgian currency, and most people here seem to speak all three languages – plus English and French. Maastricht is also the political and cultural centre of the region. Students from the city's three colleges make up quite a proportion of the population, and concerts and theatres are never in short supply.

The core of the city spreads out from the west bank of the River Maas and is bounded by its

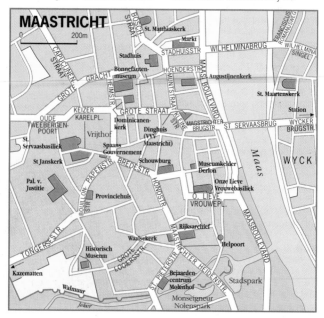

tributary, the River Jeker, to the south. Most visitors arrive at the station in the Wijk district, on the opposite, eastern bank. From here it is a short walk down Stationstraat into Wycker Brugstraat and across the river into the centre. The interesting streets of the city centre, many of them pedestrianised and lined with smart shops, converge on the huge open space of the **Vrijthof**, the main square. In contrast, the narrow old streets running south from this square lead down to the old fortifications, the River Jeker and an extensive area of peaceful parkland – a different world altogether from the bustling centre.

◆◆
BONNEFANTENMUSEUM (Good Children's Museum)
Dominikanerplein 5
Despite its name, this museum has nothing to do with children. Its name derives from the fact that the collection used to be housed in a convent belonging to the Order of the Sepulchre, whose nuns were known as Les Bons Enfants (the Good Children). That convent now holds the library of Limburg's university, and the collection has moved to this modern building, just off the Vrijthof. The material on display includes some fascinating archaeological pieces dating from Roman times, and there is even a piece of the bridge which gave the town its name (*Mosae Trajectum* – Maas Crossing).
The collection of paintings includes works by Brueghel,

Rubens and Bernard van Orley, as well as a number of regional painters and sculptors of the 17th and 18th centuries, and a Virgin and Child by Filippino Lippi.
Open: Tue–Fri 10.00–17.00hrs, Sat, Sun 11.00–17.00hrs.

◆◆
HELPOORT (Hell Gate)
Junction of Het Bat and Sint Bernardusstraat
The graphically named Hell Gate is not as sinister as it sounds – this is a well preserved city gate, the oldest to have survived in the Netherlands. It dates to 1229, and is attached to a stretch of the city's 16th-century bastions. On the opposite side of the River Jeker, in front of the gate, are the outer ramparts, and beyond that quiet parks line the south bank of the river.

◆
KAZEMETTEN (Casemates)
Waldeck Park
Waldeck Park lies in the southwestern corner of the city, just beyond the ramparts. The galleries were excavated during the 16th to19th centuries and run for about 16 miles (10km) round the town. Maastricht was besieged on 21 separate occasions during this troubled period, and the underground passages were invaluable for disguising troop movements so as to mount surprise attacks. Near the entrance is a bronze statue of d'Artagnan, the romantically immortalised musketeer and hero of Alexander Dumas' novel, who was reputed to have been killed here in 1673.

Choosing from the blooms

◆
MARKT

Though the cafés and shops of Markt are not as grand as those of Vrijthof, this is still an important central square. The 17th-century Stadhuis (Town Hall) presides over the square, and the carillon rings out from its bell tower at regular intervals throughout the day. Huge crowds of local people, swelled by Belgian visitors from Liège and Germans from Aachen, flock to the big general market that is held in the square on Wednesday and Friday mornings.

◆
MUSEUMKELDER DERLON
Plankstraat 21

This museum in the basement of the Derlon Hotel consists of interesting Roman remains, which were discovered when the hotel was built. The remains, dating to the 2nd

century AD, consist of a section of a Roman road, part of a temple to Jupiter, and various other artefacts.
Open: Sun 13.00–17.00hrs.

◆◆
ONZE LIEVE VROUWEBASILIEK
(Basilica of Our Lady)
Vrouweplein

One of the oldest buildings in Maastricht, this stately church was built on Roman foundations and dates to around AD1000. The remarkable west front, flanked by two turrets, gives the church a solid and impenetrable air. Once inside, however, the delicate Romanesque frescos in the apse and the lively sculptures on the capitals lend a touch of lightness. The treasury has a small display of vestments, paintings and reliquaries, including a beautiful 11th-century enamel box.

◆
ST JANSKERK
(St John's Church)
Vrijthof

St John's stands alongside St Servaaskerk on the west side of the main square, but cannot compete with its overpowering neighbour. It has some interesting medieval murals, but the main reason for visiting is to climb the 15th-century tower for excellent views.

◆◆
ST SERVAASBASILIEK
(Basilica of St Servatius)
Sint Servaas Klooster

The magnificent Romanesque apse and east end of this church dominate one side of the main city square. This part of the huge edifice dates from the early 13th century, and shelters an even older crypt which dates to around AD950. Within this crypt you will find the tomb of St Servatius, who became the first Bishop of Maastricht in AD382. The basilica has recently been restored, and visitors can admire the brightly painted 13th-century royal portal, and the richly decorated Gothic vaulting.

The treasury has an extensive collection of fine religious antiquities, paintings, and ivory work. Perhaps most appealing are a number of relics of St Servatius himself, including his crosier, his gold pectoral cross, his beautiful glass beaker and a reliquary with reliefs illustrating the life of the saint.

Accommodation

Beaumont, Wycker Brugstraat 2 (tel: (043) 254433). Five-star, 85 rooms; a neat and well-furnished hotel in this popular street.

Bergère, Stationsstraat 40 (tel: (043) 251651). Three-star, 40 rooms. The building dates from 1886, and the hotel, opened as recently as 1991, is smart, efficient and comfortable with its own restaurant/café. Very good value.

Du Casque, Helmstraat 14 (tel: (043) 214343). Four-star, 43 rooms; overlooking the Vrijthof, the hotel is bright and central, with moderate accommodation.

Derlon; Onze Lieve Vrouweplein 6 (tel: (043) 216770). Four-star, 42 rooms; a compact, smart hotel in the centre of town, with an unusual museum of Roman remains in the basement – comfortable but expensive.

De l'Empereur, Stationsstraat 2 (tel: (043) 213838). Four-star, 80 rooms; a comfortable, well-equipped hotel with a smart brasserie/café.

De Poshoorn, Stationsstraat 47 (tel: (043) 217334). Two-star, 10 rooms; simple, cosy and inexpensive hotel.

Eating Out

Maastricht claims to have more bars, restaurants and cafés than there are days in the year, serving every kind of cuisine, so there is no shortage of choice. The cheaper establishments are to be found in the lively streets of the Stoks quarter around Onze Lieve Vrouweplein, and there are plenty of bars selling tempting snacks around Vrijthof.

Excursions from Maastricht

Just over one mile (2km) south of the city centre is **Sint Pietersberg**, a sandstone hill which has been quarried since Roman times for building materials. As a result the hill is now honeycombed with man-made cave systems, and it is a popular tourist attraction. In total there are about 125 miles (200km) of passages, some up to 50 feet (15m) high. They were used in World War II as an escape route between Holland and Belgium. A fort on the hill was built in the early 18th century; now a restaurant, this is a good spot just to sit and enjoy the view. Tours depart daily from the Fort of St Pieter restaurant at 15.00hrs.

LIMBURG

THORN

This picturesque little village right on the Belgian border is full of beautiful white-washed cottages and farmhouses. Cobbled streets add to its charm, but the major attraction here is the outstanding abbey church in the centre of the village.

ABDIJKERK
(Abbey Church)

The abbey was founded at the end of the 10th century by Count Ansfrey and his wife Hilsondis. Unusually, the abbey housed both canons and canonesses in one establishment, many of them the sons and daughters of the local nobility. It was a thriving religious centre until dissolved by invading French revolutionary troops in 1797. The interior of the church is well worth seeing. The oldest part is the 12th-century Romanesque crypt at the west end, while the Gothic crypt of the east end is particularly fascinating, if a little grim, for its glass-topped coffins which contain the mummified remains of a canon and canoness. Most of the church was built in Gothic style in the 13th century, but the prevailing atmosphere is baroque, thanks to the profuse 17th-century decoration of the chapels.

VALKENBURG

Located in the middle of the wooded Guel valley this is one of the most visited spots in Limburg. The beauty of the surrounding countryside draws holidaymakers from all over Europe. There is plenty to see and do, though the attractions may not be to everyone's taste; there are caves to explore, a ruined castle, a modern spa centre, and a replica of the shrine at Lourdes.

GEMEENTEGROT
Cauberg

This vast man-made cave system stretches for 47 miles (75km) inside the marlstone hills around Valkenburg, quarried for centuries for their building stone. The stone is soft and easily carved, and hardens on exposure to the air. The temperature inside the caves is a constant 11°C (32°F) – chilly in summer but warm in the cold depths of winter. Taking advantage of this, local people would often amuse themselves in winter by visiting the caves to paint and carve the walls. American soldiers, wintering here in 1944, have also left their mark. The guided tour takes in the most interesting of these sculptures and cave paintings, which date back to the 15th century and include everything from family crests to dinosaurs and abstract designs carved by art students in the 1960s.
Open: Apr–Nov, daily 09.00–17.00hrs.

LOURDESGROT
Cauberg

This replica of the French shrine at Lourdes was created in 1926. Open all year, it attracts numerous Catholic pilgrims seeking a cure for various ills.

THERMAE 2000
This ultra-modern centre in the hills above Valkenburg is housed under a huge glass pyramid – so you can swim in the bubbling pools while looking out to beautiful woodland and hills. The pools are fed by naturally warm mineral-rich waters from nearby springs. All sorts of different treatments are on offer, including Turkish, Swedish, Roman and German-style baths.
Open: daily 09.00–23.00hrs.

◆

VALKENBURG (Falcon Castle)
Grendelplein
The castle which gave Valkenburg its name stands on a peak above the main street. Built in the 13th century, it was partly demolished in 1672 and is now being restored. The remains include a chapel and arsenal, and the entrance to a network of secret tunnels which were used as an escape route in times of siege.
Open: Apr–Nov, daily 10.00–18.00hrs.

◆

VENLO
Venlo's main claim to fame is its location at the centre of the large market gardening area of central Limburg – as you approach the town you will pass row after row of hothouses. The speciality of the region is white asparagus, and the production of tomatoes, mushrooms and flowers is also an important source of trade. It is worth venturing into the centre of town, both to sample the

produce and to visit a couple of the town's museums. The **Goltziusmuseum** on Goltziusstraat illustrates the history of the region through a series of period rooms furnished in the styles of the 16th to 18th centuries. There is also a comprehensive collection of 19th-century kitchen utensils. The **Van Bommel-Van Dammuseum** on Deken van Oppensingel houses temporary exhibitions by contemporary artists.

VENRAY

Venray, in the northern part of Limburg, is another important centre for market gardening. It is best known as the site of some of the fiercest battles of World War II, which took place in the woods between Venray and neighbouring Overloon.

The cobbled streets of Thorn

◆◆◆
NATIONAL OORLOGS EN VERZETSMUSEUM

(National War and Resistance Museum)

This extraordinary museum is formed from the original battlefield where Allied forces fought German tank troops for three weeks in October 1944, resulting in thousands of causalties. The aim was to force an early end to the war by cutting off the strategic corridor, known as 'Hell Highway', which was used by the Germans to transport troops and supplies through the Netherlands and into Belgium. The museum consists of two parts. Outdoors, a well-marked trail leads you round the battlefield which is littered with the machinery of the war – tanks, aeroplanes, a V1 flying bomb, bridges and armoured cars. In the indoor section of the museum the course of the war is explained and illustrated with contemporary documents, posters and photographs.
Open: Jun–Aug, daily 10.00–17.00hrs.

Paleis Het Loo

GELDERLAND

Gelderland is the largest of the twelve provinces of the Netherlands. Rivers divide the province neatly into three separate areas, each with its own distinctive character. The northwest, above the Rijn (Rhine), is known as the Veluwe, meaning Bad Land. The region derives its name from the huge expanses of sandy heathland, which are not fertile enough to support crops. There is, however, plenty for the visitor to see, including the wooded Hoge Veluwe National Park and its outstanding Kröller-Müller Museum.

The southwest, between the Rijn and the Waal, is called the Betuwe – Good Land – because of its fertile soils, which support numerous orchards and market gardens. Finally the Achterhoek (literally 'Back Corner') stretches southeast to the German border; a beautiful region of flower meadows, streams and orchards watered by the IJssel.

APELDOORN

Located in the middle of the Veluwe region, Apeldoorn is known as the 'garden city' because of its numerous parks. These are of recent creation – until the 1960s, Apeldoorn was a small moorland village, but with the relocation here of many civil servants and government departments from Amsterdam and Den Haag, the population has grown to some 140,000. The centre is modern and not particularly attractive, but the Paleis Het Loo is a must.

◆◆◆
PALEIS HET LOO
About 1 mile (2km) north of Apeldoorn
This outstanding royal palace, dating from 1685, was originally built for Prince William III before he came to the throne of England. It continued to be a favourite residence of the Dutch royal family until 1975, after which extensive restoration and refurbishment was carried out. The palace was opened in 1984 as a national museum, showing the historical and social significance of the royal House of Orange within the Netherlands.
The gardens are superb, modelled on those of Versailles (though not as extensive). The low box hedges, flower beds and gravelled walkways form intricate patterns which look particularly impressive when viewed from the upper rooms of the palace.
Open: Tue–Sun 10.00–17.00hrs.

ARNHEM

The capital of Gelderland province, Arnhem is a lively city whose numerous parks and tree-lined avenues break up the predominantly modern buildings. The town is famous for the World War II battle, known as 'Operation Market Garden' and immortalised in the film *A Bridge Too Far*, during which most of the old city was destroyed. There are plenty of reminders of the battle in the nearby war cemeteries and the Airborne Museum. On a happier note, Arnhem has an outstanding open-air museum

illustrating rural life and architecture through the ages.

◆◆
AIRBORNE MUSEUM HARTENSTEIN
Oosterbeek, 5 miles (8km) west of Arnhem
This museum traces the disastrous events of Operation Market Garden through models and audio-visual presentations. In September 1944 the Allied forces aimed to take the strategic Rhine bridges outside Arnhem, invade Germany and so end the war. The ambitious plan involved flying troops into Arnhem by parachute, but they found the bridges strongly defended, and heavy casualties resulted. Before the battle began, the Airborne Commander, General Browning, warned that: 'We might be going a bridge too far', and this memorable phrase was used as the title of Cornelis Ryann's book about the battle, and the subsequent film. The museum's collection of photographs, weapons and uniforms brings home the scale of the Allied defeat and leaves little to the imagination.
From the museum, trails lead to various memorials and battle sites, including the Oosterbeek Military Cemetary.
Open: Mon–Sat 11.00–17.00hrs, Sun 12.00–17.00hrs.

◆
GEMEENTEMUSEUM (Municipal Museum)
Utrechtseweg 87
This museum gives you a good background to the history and archaeology of Gelderland province, and helps you

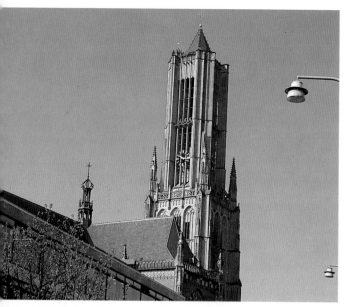

Arnhem's Grote Kerk

appreciate the area as seen
through the eyes of artists from
the 16th to19th centuries.
Temporary exhibitions of
modern Dutch art are held in
the museum throughout the
year.
Open: Tue–Sat 10.00–17.00hrs,
Sun 11.00–17.00hrs.

◆
GROTE KERK
Kerkplein
This church dates to 1452, but
the tower, destroyed in the
battle of 1944, has been
faithfully rebuilt in the original
Gothic style, with its unusual
figures on the buttresses. The
tower rises to 305 feet (93m)
and offers extensive views from
the summit.

◆◆◆
NEDERLANDS OPENLUCHTMUSEUM (Netherlands Open-Air Museum)
*Schelmseweg, 2 miles (3km)
north*
This outstanding museum, set in
109 acres (44ha) of wooded
parkland, shows how the Dutch
people have traditionally
lived and worked over the
centuries.
Authentic houses, windmills and
farms have been restored and
furnished with traditional items.
Houses from different regions
of the Netherlands are grouped
together in village units to
emphasise differences in styles
and costumes.
Open: Apr–Oct, Mon–Fri
09.00–17.00hrs, Sat, Sun
10.00–17.00hrs.

◆◆◆
HET NATIONALE PARK DE HOGE VELUWE ✓

Entrances at Schaarsbergen, Otterloo and Hoenderloo
The Hoge Veluwe National Park begins some 4 miles (6km) north of Arnhem and is the largest nature reserve in the Netherlands, covering around 13,750 acres (5,500ha). About half of this area is heathland, the rest of Scots pine and deciduous woodland. Visitors can drive, walk or bicycle (cycles are supplied free at the park entrance) around this beautiful park, enjoying the immense variety of plants and wildlife. A good place to start your explorations is in the middle of the park, at the **Aanschouw Visitors' Centre**, which tells you all about the park's history, development and wildlife (there is also a café). The park was once the private estate of Willem Kröller and his wife, Hélène Müller. It was bequeathed to the nation in 1934, with an outstanding collection of art. This is now housed in the **Rijksmuseum**, located right in the heart of the park in an exceptional woodland setting. Effective use of light and space makes the museum a delight to visit, and its pictures are displayed to their best advantage. The range is wide and includes 278 paintings by Van Gogh, along with works by Giacometti, Mondrian, Goos, Toorop, Picasso and many other 19th and 20th-century artists. In 1960 an outdoor Sculpture Park was added which cleverly surrounds the main gallery. About 90 sculptures, including works by Hepworth, Moore and Rodin, are gracefully arranged among the trees and shrubs. To the north of the park is the **Jachthuis St Hubertus** (St Hubert's Hunting Lodge), built in 1914 for the Kröller-Müllers by the Amsterdam School architect, H P Berlage. Visitors are given guided tours around this huge and rather incongruous building, set in a lovely position beside a lake. The village of Otterloo on the western edge of the park has a number of hotels and restaurants, and makes a good base from which to explore the area. Also in the village is the **Tegelmuseum** (Tile Museum) which has a large and interesting collection of decorated ceramic tiles dating from the 14th century to the present day.
Open: park, daily 08.00 to sunset; Kröller-Müller Museum (Rijksmuseum), Tue–Sat 10.00–17.00hrs, Sun 11.00–17.00hrs (Nov–Mar 13.00–17.00hrs).

NIJMEGEN

Nijmegen is one of the oldest towns in the Netherlands. It was founded by the Romans in AD105, who called it *Novio Magus* (New Market). Built on seven hills overlooking the River Waal, the town has had a turbulent history. Much of the town was destroyed during the fierce fighting that took place in the final months of World War II. Even so, there is still plenty to see. The **Waag** (Weigh-house)

in the centre of Grote Markt is a
fine example of highly coloured
Dutch Renaissance style.
Opposite is the imposing 13th-
century Gothic **St Stevenskerk**.
Nijmegen has an unusual
number of parks, where visitors
mingle with students from the
Catholic University.

◆

BEVRIJDINGSMUSEUM
(Liberation Museum)
Keizer Traianusplein 35
This museum reconstructs
Nijmegen's role in the final
stages of World War II through
audio-visual materials, maps
and photographs.
Open: Mon–Sat 10.00–17.00hrs,
Sun 12.00–17.00hrs.

◆

NIJMEEGS MUSEUM
'COMMANDERIE VAN ST JAN'
Fransplaats
This building dates back to
1196, when the Knights of St
John built a hospice on the site.
The hospice suffered war
damage earlier this century,
which necessitated substantial
reconstruction, and the building
now houses a museum
covering Nijmegen's history,
including a collection of
paintings of the town and the
surrounding area.
Open: Mon–Sat 10.00–17.00hrs,
Sun 13.00–17.00hrs.

◆◆

RIJKSMUSEUM KAM
Museum Kamstraat 45
This excellent museum contains
a wealth of archaeological
material, mostly Roman, found
during excavations in the town.
Open: Tue–Sat 10.00–17.00hrs,
Sun 13.00–17.00hrs.

ZUTPHEN

Zutphen was granted its city
charter in 1190, making it one
of the oldest towns in
Gelderland. It was strategically
important in early territorial
battles, hence the substantial
remains of fortifications
between the Grote Kerk and the
River IJssel. Although Zutphen
was, in theory, easy to defend –
being protected by the rivers
IJssel and Berkel and
surrounded by marshy ground
– it was captured by the
Spanish during the Dutch Revolt
and its citizens massacred. It
again suffered damage during
World War II, but its historic
buildings have been well
restored.

◆◆

GROTE KERK
(ST WALBURGISKERK)
's Gravenhof
Originally built in the 13th
century, this church was
extended and then restored
after suffering damage in World
War II. The highlight is the
beautiful 16th-century library in
the Chapter House, which has
remained more or less in its
original state, complete with
wooden reading desks to which
the printed books and
illuminated manuscripts were
chained to guard against theft.

◆

STEDELIJK MUSEUM
(Municipal Museum)
This museum has an interesting
collection of clocks, silver and
chinaware, and other pieces
relevant to the town's history.
Open: Tue–Fri 11.00–17.00hrs,
Sat–Sun 13.30–17.00hrs.

FLEVOLAND

The province of Flevoland is the latest addition to the Netherlands and consists entirely of land reclaimed from the sea since the end of World War II. The first inhabitants began to arrive in 1967, and Flevoland was given provincial status in 1986. Not surprisingly, the region is extremely flat, and the main industries here are horticulture and agriculture. The capital is **Lelystad**, named after Dr Cornelius Lely, the engineer who initiated the Zuiderzee reclamation scheme. The story of this ambitious project, which led to the creation of Flevoland, is told at the **Informatiecentrum Nieuw Land** in the town (*open*: Apr–Oct, daily 10.00–17.00hrs; Nov–Mar, Mon–Fri 10.00–17.00hrs).

Lelystad and the other towns of Flevoland are modern and functional, lacking the charm of the older parts of the country. However, as an engineering feat, the creation of these polders has been an outstanding achievement and a major boost to the agricultural economy.

Newly reclaimed farmland, typical of Flevoland province.

OVERIJSSEL

The province of Overijssel consists of two regions, which are divided by the north–south motorway that links Zwolle and Meppel. To the west is an area of interesting villages and numerous small lakes created by peat-cutting activities. Spread out over a wide area, the lakes are now extremely popular with boating enthusiasts. One of the main yachting centres is **Blokzijl**, to the western side of the lakes, a charming small town, with a mixture of thatched cottages and grander 17th-century houses.

The eastern half of the province is more industrial. Historically this was a major centre for textile production, and the region underwent a mini Industrial Revolution in the early 19th century when power looms were imported from England. Today, electronics and light engineering are of equal importance.

GIETHOORN

Giethoorn stands on the western edge of the lakeland area. The name of this fascinating village is a corruption of *Geytenhorn* (Goats' Horns), from the discovery of thousands of goats' horns buried in the peat, probably the remains of wild goats drowned by flooding in ancient times.

The village was founded in the 13th century by a strict religious sect of flagellants, persecuted in most countries, who managed to find a refuge

NORTH HOLLAND

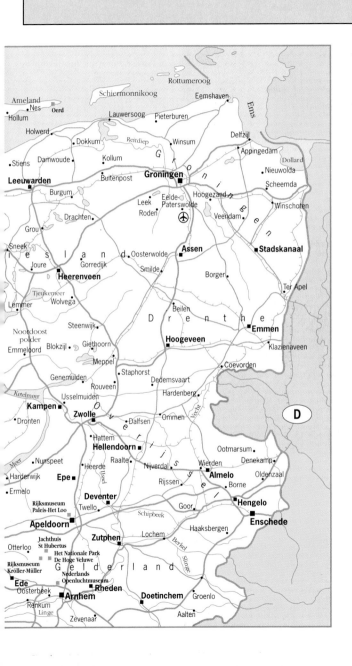

Exploring the canals of Giethoorn in a 'punter'

the village, though there is parking on the outskirts. From here you can either take an organised boat tour or hire your own flat-bottomed boat, called a *punter*. Cycles are also available for hire; but travelling by boat is much more fun.

◆◆◆
WHAT TO SEE IN GIETHOORN

Giethoorn is a very unusual and picturesque place which has inevitably been compared with Venice, though this is a very homely Dutch version. The thatched cottages all stand in pretty gardens and are reached over wooden hump-backed bridges. Visitors can tie up the *punters* alongside Binnenpad, where there are three small museums: one has a collection of precious stones, another displays musical instruments and the third has an exhibition of shells. The special Giethoorn *punters* are made in the nearby Schreur shipyard.

Accommodation

There are some very basic hotels in Giethoorn, but a better base for the region is the following hotel in Blokzijl: **Kaatje bij de Sluis**, Zuiderstraat 1 (tel: (05272) 1833). Four-star, 8 rooms; a comfortable, attractive hotel with a very good restaurant.

KAMPEN

Kampen is a striking town located on the river IJssel, which forms the southern boundary of Overijssel province. Kampen was once a prosperous port but the closing of the Zuiderzee (to create the

here. In order to raise the money to pay rent to the local landlord, they cut and sold the peat. Gradually the peat cuttings filled with water, creating a string of small lakes. The lakes were then linked by canals, which were dug for transport. Now the only way to travel around the area is by boat. No cars are allowed into

IJsselmeer) has left it without any access to the open sea. Instead it has become a river port, with many reminders of its 16th-century prosperity in the lovely gabled façades of its older buildings.

◆
GOTISCHE HUIS (Gothic House)
Oudestraat 158
This gracious 15th-century house, originally built for a wealthy merchant, now houses a museum which covers the history of Kampen.
Open: mid Jun–mid Sep, Tue–Sat 11.00–17.00hrs, Sun 13.00–17.00hrs.

◆
STADHUIS (Town Hall)
Oudestraat 133
Kampen's town hall consists of an 18th-century wing and an older building, called the Oude Raadhuis, that dates to 1543. Within the latter is the Magistrate's Hall, with a fine Dutch carved Renaissance chimneypiece and some excellent carved woodwork.
Open: May–Sep, Mon–Thu 11.00–16.00hrs, Sat 14.00–17.00hrs.

TWENTE

Twente is the industrial conurbation in the eastern part of Overijssel province, an area with its own dialect and culture, influenced by its proximity to the German border. The region's main town, **Enschede**, has two very good museums, one covering art and the other the local textile industry, but the most rewarding destination is the lovely town of Ootmarsum.

◆◆
OOTMARSUM
122 miles (20km) north of Enschede
This attractive town is surrounded by low wooded hills, which form a fitting backdrop to the numerous old, beautifully renovated timber houses. These, together with the town's well-restored Renaissance façades, give a good impression of the atmosphere and appearance of the town as it must have been in the 18th century.
Ootmarsum can be crowded in summer, and is best visited out of season when you can fully appreciate the beauties of this charming place.

ZWOLLE

Zwolle is the capital of Overijssel, and the compact heart of this beautiful old town is almost circular in shape, completely surrounded by water and protected by 17th-century ramparts. The town is easily explored on foot, but for something different, you could hire a pedal boat (*pedaloe*) for a leisurely circuit of the moat.

◆
PROVINCIAAL OVERIJSSELS MUSEUM
Voorstraat 34
The Overijssel Provincial Museum is housed in a handsome 16th-century mansion with period furnishings that illustrate the life of a wealthy merchant in the region's heyday. The museum traces Zwolle's rise to prosperity as an important town within the Hanseatic League,

trading with Germany and the Baltic ports, and its decline in the 17th century, when Amsterdam took its place as the pre-eminent port in the Netherlands.

Open: Tue–Sat 10.00–17.00hrs, Sun 14.00–17.00hrs.

Excursions from Zwolle

Some 10 miles (16km) north of Zwolle are the villages of **Staphorst** and **Rouveen**, together forming one very long and almost continuous settlement. These villages are renowned for their traditional thatched buildings and the strict religious observance of the inhabitants. The villagers reject

Grazing in Emmen's zoo

many of the trappings and luxuries of modern life – and the traditional black costumes are worn as a matter of course and specifically not for the benefit of tourists. It is considered impolite to photograph them, and visitors are asked to be sensitive to the ways of these unusual communities.

DRENTHE

Drenthe province has long been something of a backwater, a sparsely populated region of peat bogs and moorland. Development did not begin until the 11th century, and the province still has a peaceful atmosphere. Few visitors come here but those who do fall in

love with its thatched farmhouses and rural charm. The two main towns of Assen and Emmen are not large - their joint population is about 140,000.

Assen, the provincial capital, is the older town. Its highlight is the **Drents Museum** (Drenthe Museum), located at Brink 1–5, which gives you a good idea of the history and geology of the area. Assen is also renowned for the International Motorcycling TT Grand Prix which takes place in June.

Emmen, the larger town, is essentially a modern industrial centre with not much to see and do, although the zoo in **Noorder Dierenpark**, located in the middle of the town, is worth visiting. The zoo is modern in concept, with large areas of 'savannah' where the animals live in as natural an environment as possible. Emmen is a good base for exploring the prehistoric *hunebeds* (burial mounds) that dot the surrounding moorland. The VVV tourist office in Emmen sells maps showing their location. The nearest to the town centre is the well-signposted Emmerdennen Hunebed, reached by following Boslaan from the station for about half a mile (1km).

Some 7 miles (11km) east of Emmen is another star attraction, an open-air museum called **Veenmuseumdorp 't Aole Compas** which recreates the appearance of a 19th-century peat-mining village, including exhibitions on the extraction of peat for use as fuel and as a building material.

FRIESLAND

Friesland province is most easily reached by driving north from Amsterdam to Den Oever and crossing the 19-mile (30km) Afsluitdijk. This dam, completed in 1932, separates the IJsselmeer (now a freshwater lake) from the shallow tidal Waddenzee. The long straight road across the top of the dam provides uninterrupted views of the lake and the sea, and with nothing else in sight you may feel a sense of suspended reality. You can stay at the café half way across, with its viewing platform, if you are feeling mesmerised. Otherwise, land and reality return when you enter the province of Friesland, just south of Harlingen.

Friesland and the neighbouring province of Groningen are both noted for their ancient *terp* villages – so called because they are built on *terpen* (mounds of earth) to avoid the frequent flooding. Perhaps more than any other Dutch province, Friesland is fiercely proud of its heritage, and Friesians even have their own distinct language – so you will sometimes see bilingual road signs.

One way of understanding the history and culture of the province is to take the Aldfaers Erf Route (Heritage Route). This 13 mile (20km) trail takes in a number of pretty little villages, each of which has a museum covering aspects of traditional life in Friesland. The route will also give you a taste of typical Friesland scenery: streams running though the green meadows, grazed by black and white Friesian cows, and beautiful farmhouses with red-tiled roofs. The route starts at Bolsward, and is clearly marked.

HARLINGEN

Harlingen is a very attractive town with a busy working port. Ferries depart from here to the Wadden Islands of Vlieland and Terschelling, and you will see fishing trawlers, cargo boats and barges tied up along the two old harbours of **Noorderhaven** and **Zuiderhaven**. Some of these old vessels are designed especially for sailing on the shallow waters of the Waddenzee, which stretches from here to the Wadden Islands. Almost the whole of the docks area between the two harbours is designated as a conservation area, for its fine gabled houses are interspersed

Friesland's lake district

with warehouses, many dating to the 17th and 18th centuries.

GEMEENTEMUSEUM HANNEMAHUIS (Municipal Museum)
Voorstraat 56
Harlingen's town museum is housed in an 18th-century house built by the Hannema family, local merchants. The displays cover the whaling industry, which was important to the region in the 17th century, shipping and local crafts – notably the beautiful hand-painted tiles that were produced in the town up to 1933, an industry that has very recently been revived.

Accommodation
Anna Casparii, Noorderhaven 67–71 (tel: (05178) 12065). Three-star, 15 rooms; set in a good position on this pretty harbour.
Zeezicht Zuiderhaven 1 (tel: (05178) 12536). Two-star, 25 rooms; a friendly, simple hotel on the harbour junction; some rooms have sea views.

HINDELOOPEN

Hindeloopen is one of the picturesque little towns that feature in Friesland's famous Elfstedentocht, the 'Eleven Towns Race'. This skating marathon takes place in winter if the canals freeze sufficiently to support ice skaters. The race is one of the most gruelling events of all sports, and the participants have to be extremely fit. The town is also famous for its hand-painted furniture, which is widely sold in the town centre.

◆
GEMEENTEMUSEUM HIDDE NIJLAND STICHTING
Dijkweg 1
This museum has a good collection of old furniture, decorated with painted flowers and foliage on a white, red or green background, the speciality of local furniture makers since the 16th century. The furniture and the local costumes on display both show the influence of Scandinavia, a reminder that Hindeloopen once had extensive trade contacts with the Baltic ports.
Open: Mar–Oct, Mon–Sat 10.00–17.00hrs, Sun 13.30–17.00hrs .

◆
SCHAATS MUSEUM
(Skating Museum)
This little museum in a furniture shop displays mementoes of the Elfstedentocht ('Eleven Towns Race') skating marathons. This gruelling race began in 1890 and takes place every five years or so, depending on the weather. If the temperature drops low enough for long enough in winter to freeze the canal network in Friesland, then the race is on. The route measures 125 miles (200km), starting from the provincial capital, Leeuwarden, and ending at Dokkum. Of the 17,000 or so competitors who start the race, fewer than 300 will complete the route. The course has been completed in under seven hours. The race is watched closely on TV, and the winner is assured of instant fame throughout the Netherlands.

LEEUWARDEN

Leeuwarden is the cultural and economic capital of Friesland, and the city, spread out over a large area, presents a rather haphazard mixture of old and new buildings. A bronze statue of a Friesian cow stands sentinel at the entrance to the town and this, in many ways, is an appropriate symbol: the Friday cattle market is one of the biggest in the country and the town is the centre of the thriving dairy industry.
Leeuwarden was also the birthplace of the notorious Mata Hari (whose real name was Margarethe Geertruide Zella), the seductive dancer who was accused of being a German spy and shot in 1917

◆◆
FRIES MUSEUM
Turfmarkt 24
This excellent museum provides an exhaustive account of Friesland, including its social, political, cultural and economic background. Collections of costumes, furniture, and reconstructions of old shops bring the history of the province vividly to life.
Open: Tue–Sat 10.00–17.00hrs, Sun 13.00–17.00hrs.

◆◆
GEMEENTELIJKMUSEUM HET PRINCESSEHOF
Grote Kerkstraat 9–15
This museum was built as a palace in 1650 and acquired later by the aristocratic Stadholder Willem Friso, who named it after his wife, Princess Marie-Louise of Hesse-Cassel. Some of the rooms are

FRIESLAND

decorated in the style of the mid-18th century, but the majority of the museum consists of a huge and remarkable collection of ceramics and tiles from all over the world, dating from 200BC to the 20th century. Many of the best pieces on display are Chinese and Japanese porcelain imported by the Dutch East India Company from the beginning of the 17th century. Equally fascinating are the hand-painted Dutch tiles dating back to the 15th century, when Italian potters introduced majolica production techniques to the Netherlands.
Open: Mon–Sat 10.00–17.00hrs, Sun 14.00–17.00hrs .

Accommodation

De Pauw, Stationsweg 10 (tel: (058) 123651). One-star, 30 rooms; central but very simple.
Oranje, Stationsweg 4 (tel: (058) 126241). Four-star, 76 rooms; a very comfortable hotel with a choice of restaurants.

MAKKUM

Makkum is renowned for its hand-painted pottery which the inhabitants claim is superior to Delft. The **Friese Aardewerkmuseum** (Friesian Pottery Museum) in the 17th-century weigh-house exhibits a good range of local Makkum wares. **Tichelaar**, on Turfmarkt, has been making Makkum pottery for more than 300 years and the company is now entitled to call its products Koninklijke (Royal) Makkum. Local clays are still used, and the techniques of firing, hand-painting and glazing have

changed little over the centuries. Here you can watch potters and painters at work, and admire and buy a range of products in the Royal Makkum showrooms.

SNEEK

Sneek (pronounced 'Snake') lies at the heart of Friesland's lake district and is very popular with sailing and watersports enthusiasts, especially during the Sneek Week regatta which takes place at the beginning of August. Visitors can rent sailing and motor boats, or join boat excursions to the lakes at Oosterkade, the quay to the east of the town centre. The most attractive part of Sneek lies around the Renaissance **Waterpoort**, a beautiful gate adjoining the remains of the old town ramparts. The **Stadhuis** (Town Hall), on Marktstraat, has a remarkable rococo façade, and other fine gabled buildings are spread around the town.

♦♦
FRIES SCHEEPVAART MUSEUM
(Friesian Maritime Museum)

Kleinzand 14
This is a must for everyone fascinated by navigation and things nautical. The well-displayed collection includes model ships illustrating the different forms of boats used for inland transport, fishing and warfare, as well as pleasure craft, from the 17th century onwards. One room is devoted to the local Visser family who made a fortune exporting eels for sale on the streets of 18th-century London.

Open: Mon–Sat 10.00–12.00 and 13.30–17.00hrs.

Accommodation

Bonnema en Van Beek, Stationstraat 62–6 (tel: (05150) 13175).Three-star, 13 rooms. **Hanenburg**, Wijde Noorderhorne 2 (tel: (05150) 12570). Three-star, 12 rooms; with a restaurant.

Excursions from Sneek

About 10 miles (16km) south of Sneek is **Sloten**, a delightful fortified town close to its own lake. This is said to be the smallest town in Friesland, and it consists of little more than a central canal lined by cobbled streets and gabled houses. Another town worth visiting is **Workum**, about 10 miles (16km) southwest of Sneek. The pretty town has some fine 17th and 18th-century façades, specially around the main square. The town used to be at the centre of the eel trade, and this is explained in the small museum in the Waag (weigh-house).

GRONINGEN (PROVINCE)

Groningen is the least visited province of the Netherlands but is worth exploration. The motorway system does not reach this far north, which only adds to the charm since the rural roads are quiet and more than adequate. The landscape is similar to that of Friesland, consisting predominantly of flat green pasture and raised villages built on mounds which are called *terpen* in Friesland but *wierden* in Groningen. The best district for touring lies northwest of the capital. Here

are numerous unspoiled villages that present a picture of old rural Holland. Each village has a church, sometimes sitting on a mound, and a bell-tower with its characteristic saddleback roof. The tower is often the only part of the church you can see from a distance as it pokes above a protective circle of trees. Peat farming is another local speciality, and the landscape bears the marks and relics of this centuries-old industry.

If you drive to the northwestern tip of the province, around the estuary of the river Ems, you will see how the Dutch are continuing to reclaim land, with the new port of Eemshaven emerging from the surrounding polders.

GRONINGEN

Groningen is the capital city of its own province, and the main administrative and intellectual centre of the northern Dutch provinces as a whole. Despite being some 15 miles (24km)

Martinikerk tower, Groningen

from the coast, Groningen is linked to the North Sea by the Eems Kanaal, which opened in 1876 and is capable of taking large sea-going ships. As a result Groningen has developed considerable importance as an industrial and commercial centre.

The town has a lively and youthful atmosphere thanks to the estimated 20,000 students who attend the local university. Consequently, there is no lack of lively bars and cafés, and it has a full cultural programme – one reason why the city is sometimes called 'the Amsterdam of the North'.

GRONINGER MUSEUM
Praediniussingel 59

This is an excellent place to learn about the history of the province and its people. One of the star attractions is a display of Chinese ceramics, raised in 1985 from a Dutch ship which sank in the South China Seas in 1572. The collection of paintings includes some notable works, such as Rubens' *Adoration of the Magi*, and Impressionist seascapes by the Hague School artists H W Mesdag and Isaac Israels, both of whom were born in the city. *Open:* Tue–Sat 10.00–17.00hrs, Sun 13.00–17.00hrs.

MARTINIKERK
Grote Markt

The church tower, variously known as the Martini Tower and The Old Grey Man acts as a magnet to most visitors. It was built in Gothic style in the 15th century and rises to a height of 328 feet (100m). You can climb to the top to appreciate the bell carillon and get the best view over the town. Inside the church look out for the beautifully painted 15th and 16th-century frescos depicting the Life of Christ.

NOORDELIJK SCHEEPVAARTMUSEUM (Northern Maritime Museum)
Brugstraat 24

This excellent museum is one of the best of the numerous maritime museums in the Netherlands. It is located in a pair of heavily timbered merchants' houses built in the 16th century. The displays are informative about the maritime history of northern Holland, from its beginning in the 6th century AD right up to the present day, illustrated with models and maps, and there is a series of rooms devoted to the skills of the carpenter, blacksmith, rope maker and sail maker. Apart from sea-going vessels, the museum also looks at boats designed for use on inland waterways. *Open:* Tue–Sat 10.00–17.00hrs, Sun 13.00–17.00hrs.

Excursions from Groningen

On the northern coast, seal lovers should find time to visit the **Zeehondencreche** (Seal Hospital) at Pieterburen, Hoofdstraat 94A, set up by Lenie 't Hart. This combines the care of sick seals with fundamental research – especially into the distemper-like virus which has decimated the local population of common seals.

THE WADDEN ISLANDS

The Wadden Islands (also known as the Friesian Islands) stretch in a broad arc northeastwards from the top of Noord Holland province towards the coast of Germany. On the map these islands look like a strip of land that has come adrift from the mainland and broken into irregular sized pieces. In fact the islands are part of a huge sandbank, most of which lies below the water. The bank forms a natural breakwater between the North Sea and the northern provinces of the Netherlands. In between is a huge area of shallow water known as the Waddenzee (literally 'Muddy Sea').

The average depth of the Waddenzee is 3 feet (1m) and nowhere is it deeper than 10 feet (3m), even at high tide. At low tide the sea retreats, revealing an area of mudflats covering some 1,000 square miles (2,600 sq km) which is rich in marine life and attracts large numbers of feeding birds. The islands, too, are a haven for birds and other wildlife,

especially wild flowers. There are five major islands in the group as well as a number of tiny uninhabited ones.

Good sandy beaches are another feature of these islands, and on sunny summer weekends they can be very crowded. At other times the islands are blissfully free of visitors and offer a real taste of the wild.

◆
AMELAND

The ferry to Ameland goes from Holwerd (in Friesland province) and takes about 45 minutes. Ferries depart six times daily, on average, and reservations are recommended (tel: (05191) 6111).

The ferry docks at **Nes**, one of Ameland's four villages and once an important whaling centre. Now the islanders live by cattle farming and by tourism, for Ameland is a major resort in summer; visitors come for the sandy beach, 16 miles (25km) long, which stretches

Lifeboat launching practice on the island of Ameland

THE WADDEN ISLANDS

Island home

the length of the island's northern shore.

Cars are not allowed on the island so you can either explore it on foot, by bicycle (there are several hire shops in Nes), by island bus – which does a circuit of the four main villages roughly every hour in summer – or by boat.

All four of the island's villages are part of a conservation area and retain well-preserved 17th and 18th-century houses. **Hollum**, the westernmost village, has an interesting museum giving insight into the life of the whalers. **Ballum** once had a palace that was home to the rulers of the island. There is an airport near here from which visitors can try parachute jumping. **Buren** is the smallest of the villages, equally as charming, with a 17th-century church.

Nature reserves cover a large area of the island. **Oerd** on the east of the island is the biggest, but all are well protected from tourist development and offer the chance to see a large number of birds. The VVV

tourist office supplies details of nature trails, cycle routes and accommodation on the island, ranging from hotels to camping sites.

◆
SCHIERMONNIKOOG

Ferries to Schiermonnikoog depart from Lauwersoog, in Groningen province. Ferries depart four times a day and the crossing takes 45 minutes (tel: (05193) 050). You can also reach this island by boat excursions from the neighbouring island of Ameland. Schiermonnikoog is the smallest of the inhabited islands and the most northerly. Its name means 'island of the grey monks', a reminder that it was once a monastic property. Today it is the abode of birds and the occasional common seal.

No motorised transport is allowed here, and this is the most peaceful of all the islands. The north coast consists of a long sandy beach, where nudists are welcome. Just south of this is a large nature reserve, **De Kobbeduinen**, where rare dune plants such as sea holly and horned poppy can be seen.

◆◆
TERSCHELLING

Terschelling is the second largest of the Wadden Islands and is reached by a ferry trip from Harlingen, in the province of Friesland. The regular ferry (tel: (05620) 6111) takes 90 minutes but there is also a 50-minute express service. The ferry docks at West Terschelling, the largest town and the capital of the island.

One of the unmissable features of this port is the huge **Brandaris** lighthouse overlooking the bay, which rises to 177 feet (54m). Two other villages, **Midsland** and **Hoorn**, are worth visiting and all three centres have great charm. Terschelling is renowned for its nature reserves and one of the biggest – 11,000 acres (4,400ha) in extent – is **De Boschplaat** at the east end of the island(see **Peace and Quiet**). Rich and varied vegetation and thousands of birds make this a very special place to visit.

♦♦♦
TEXEL

Texel is the largest, most southerly and most accessible of the islands. Thus it has the largest population (12,200 inhabitants) and it receives the most visitors – it can get very crowded in the height of summer. The ferry for Texel departs from Den Helder; there is an hourly service throughout the year and the crossing takes 20 minutes (no reservations but for information tel: (02220) 69600). You can take a car onto the island, but it is only 16 miles (25km) long and 6 miles (9km) wide so it is easy to get about by bike. The ferry docks at 't Horntje, from where there are buses to the main town of Den Burg. There you can hire a bicycle and pick up trail leaflets.

Texel's flat green fields are grazed by cattle and the distinctive local breed of sheep. The little huts that dot the fields are used for storing hay, and the leeward side provides the sheep with shelter from the strong easterly winds – which is why the huts all face the same direction. **Den Burg** is the main market town but **De Koog**, on the northwestern shore, is the main resort. De Koog is not particularly memorable but the long sandy beach, backed by grassy dunes, is excellent. **Cocksdorp**,

Dune landscape, Texel

on the northernmost tip of the island, also has resort facilities and a good beach. **Ecomare**, near De Koog, is an indoor water park combined with an outdoor bird and seal sanctuary. The displays here provide useful information on the island's flora and fauna. Texel is a perfect island if you enjoy swimming, cycling, walking, bird-watching and windsurfing. The island is also one of the most important bird-breeding grounds in Europe and there are numerous nature reserves (see also **Peace and Quiet**).

◆

VLIELAND

Vlieland lies between Texel and Terschelling and can be reached by a 90-minute ferry trip from Harlingen, in Friesland province (tel: (05620) 2969). The only cars allowed on the island are those of the residents, so you are likely to have a peaceful time. The ferry docks at **Oost-Vlieland** where you can hire bicycles from the VVV tourist office. There is also a bus service which runs around the island about five times a day. There is a popular marina not far from the centre of this village, but the best beaches are on the north coast. The southwestern end consists of a large sandflat called the Vliehors, which is used as a military exercise area. The east coast is best for bird-watching and walking along the well-marked nature trails.

Accommodation

There are hotels on all five islands but not a great selection. There are, however, plenty of self-catering holiday houses, bungalows and apartments to rent and numerous campsites. In summer it may be difficult to find accommodation if you have not booked in advance, especially at the weekend.

Exploring the mudflats

Peace and Quiet

Wildlife and Countryside in the Netherlands

by Paul Sterry

Introduction

Huge areas of the Netherlands have been claimed from the sea, making this, in some ways, a very un-natural country. Farming, forestry and urban expansion have also altered the 'natural' habitats.

Despite the alterations, superb locations for wildlife still remain, and many species have actually benefited from human influence. Take some bird species, for example: black-tailed godwits are common in marshy grazing pastures even on the outskirts of Amsterdam; marsh harriers breed in polders that have been seeded with reeds, and black woodpeckers have extended their range with the spread of plantation conifers.

Most of the Netherlands' wildlife is related to wetlands or coastal areas, and there are wonderful reserves and national parks. Away from the coast, extensive heathy woodlands add another dimension to the natural history interest. Most sites are within easy reach of Amsterdam.

Typical coastal habitat

De Kennemerduinen National Park

Situated on the coast 22 miles (35km) east of Amsterdam, De Kennemerduinen is an extensive area of dunes. Although managed by a waterworks company, the landscape is protected by its national park status. Access is from Bergen or Alkmaar. There are two car parks and an information centre, and footpaths allow easy access to the dune systems.

A wide range of salt-tolerant plants grow on the coast here, and away from the sea, marram grass soon colonises the shifting sands. Marsh plants are abundant in the hollows between the dunes, and wetland birds (migrant ducks in particular) favour the shallow pools, many of which are artificial.

PEACE AND QUIET

Dune Flora

Coastal dunes are home to specialised plants that are adapted to life in a hostile environment. They must be able to tolerate the effects of salt-laden winds from the sea and cope with sands that are often shifting and which contain little usable moisture. Marram grass is the classic colonising species that helps stabilise the sands. Once the sands stop moving, plants such as sea holly, yellow-horned poppy, sea kale and many others are able to establish themselves. As the dunes build up, hollows (called 'slacks') develop between them. Some contain pools of water and most remain damp for much of the year. In these areas look for exciting plants such as marsh orchids, marsh helleborines, Grass of Parnassus, round-leafed wintergreen and a curious little fern called moonwort.

Other Coastal Areas near Amsterdam

The North Sea coast of the Netherlands has many exciting wildlife locations. Among the best are the following:
Zwanenwater is a nature reserve that protects an area of dunes and freshwater pools 31 miles (50km) northwest of Amsterdam, just south of Callanstoog. The dune flora is excellent, and wildfowl and waders frequent the pools, especially during migration times in spring and autumn.

Visitors are requested to keep to the marked footpaths.
Boswachterij Schoorl Nature Reserve is an extensive area of dunes 25 miles (40km) northwest of Amsterdam. To reach it, drive to Alkmaar and continue for 7 miles (12km) to Schoorl. There is a visitor centre here as well as paths and trails. Pine plantations harbour a different range of bird species from the open dunes, and the dune flora is excellent.
Meijendel Nature Reserve is an extensive coastal area with a wide variety of habitats, ranging from dunes to marsh and woodlands. It lies 25 miles (40km) north of Rotterdam and 43 miles (70km) southeast of Amsterdam. Access is from Wassenaar, on the road from Den Haag to Haarlem. There is an information centre and several nature trails.
Duinen van Voorne Nature Reserve lies on the coast 25 miles (40km) west of Rotterdam. Entrances to the reserve are from Oostvoorne and Rockanje. As well as sand dunes, there are areas of woodland and large freshwater lakes. One of these lies close to the northern shores of Haringvliet, where it is crossed by Haringvlietdam. There are parking facilities here, and an information centre at the Oostvoorne entrance.

De Hoge Veluwe National Park

This large area of heathland and woodlands lies 6 miles (10km) northwest of Arnhem, in the south of the country. A road runs around most of the perimeter of De Hoge Veluwe and passes through Otterloo and Hoenderloo. There is access to the park at these three towns. A road network criss-crosses the area and there are numerous parking places and an information centre 3 miles (4km) east of Otterloo. De Hoge Veluwe was originally covered in natural forest vegetation, but when the woodland was cleared for agricultural purposes, poor, sandy soils were exposed, which were then colonised by heathland plants. Although large areas of open heathland still remain, patches of naturally regenerated woodland can be found and parts of the park have well established pine plantations. All the expected heathland plants can be found here, including bell heather, bilberry and purple moor grass. Special birds to look out for include hobbies and nightjars, while the wooded areas have honey buzzards and black woodpeckers. As an added attraction, De Hoge Veluwe also harbours red and roe deer, moufflon and wild boar. Every season has something to offer, but spring is best for flowers and for breeding birds.

Veluwezoom National Park

A mixture of heath and woodland covers this park, which is about 6 miles (10km) northeast of Arnhem. The woodland has both conifers and deciduous trees including oak, birch and beech. Typical heathland flowers include heathers, bog myrtle and bog asphodel. Among the woodland birds are sparrowhawks and golden orioles. In books, golden orioles are a dazzling yellow which you would think would make them very easy to spot. Not so: in the dappled shades of a woody glade they become exceptionally difficult to see. You are most likely to pinpoint one by its call – a loud, clear four-part whistle. There is an information centre as well as several car parks. A network of roads and tracks allows exploration of the park.

Swallowtail butterfly

PEACE AND QUIET

Wetland creek

Wild Boar

These ancestors of our domesticated pigs still roam wild in many parts of mainland Europe, including forested areas in the Netherlands. When full grown they are extremely bulky and forbidding animals, but they are rather shy and retiring (not surprising, since they are hunted in many regions). There can be few more endearing sights than that of a mother with half a dozen beautifully striped piglets scampering in attendance.

Brabantse Biesbosch Nature Reserve

Biesbosch is a tremendous area of wetland in the northern part of the Rhine delta; the nearest large town is Dordrecht. The reserve lies between two channels – the Bergse Mass and the Nieuwe Merwede – at the confluence where they form the Hollands Diep. Access from the north is via the bridge across the Nieuwe Merwede at Kop van 't Land. Turn right and follow the road which runs southwest along the edge of the reserve, exploring minor roads where available. The interior of the reserve can only be properly explored by boat, but most of the interesting species can be seen from the road. A range of wetland habitats can be seen here, including inundated woodland, marshes, creeks, polders and reservoirs. The area is best known for its birds; breeding species are numerous and include marsh harriers, bearded tits and night herons. In spring and autumn, a diverse range of migrating waders and wildfowl appear. Unfortunately, the creation of the Haringvliet dam across the mouth of the Rhine (near Duinen van Voorne Nature Reserve) means that the area is now no longer tidal. This will undoubtedly cause changes in the vegetation of the region.

Flevoland

This is one of the most important wildlife destinations in the Netherlands. Created by the enclosure of the Zuiderzee, the area comprises a mixture of marshes, reedbeds, channels, lakes and agricultural land. The contiguous areas of Oostelijk Flevoland and Zuidelijk Flevoland, which stretch between Naarden and Kampen, with the IJsselmeer to the northwest, are of most interest. Oostelijk Flevoland, in the northeast, is probably the best and most interesting of all.

To reach Flevoland, drive east from Amsterdam and cross to Flevoland at Naarden. Alternatively, take the road to Zwolle; and there are crossings at Harderwijk, Elburg and Kampen. The marshes, reedbeds and forestry plantations will repay the most attention, and the road from Harderwijk to Lelystad can be particularly good. There is also a nature reserve at Oostvaarderplassen (on the west side of Zuidelijk Flevoland) which has an information centre and observation tower.

What to Look Out For

In the summer, breeding species of birds include marsh harriers, spoonbills, black-tailed godwits, ruffs and many different wildfowl, including red-crested pochards and pintails. Migration time in spring and autumn can also be exciting, with waders and terns in abundance.

Many bird-watchers, however, choose to visit Flevoland in the winter months, when there arrive vast flocks of wildfowl, and in particular geese and swans. Greylag, pink-footed and white-fronted geese are abundant and there are always a few rarities such as red-breasted geese. As an added bonus, white-tailed eagles are also winter visitors – though they take their toll of the wildfowl.

Grey heron

Polders

Polders are areas of low-lying land – generally below sea level – that have been reclaimed from the sea by enclosure. The largest and best known examples are found on Flevoland. For many years after the creation of the embankments that keep out the sea, a shallow lake persists over each polder, but drainage gradually lowers the water level, and finally vast reedbeds are created by sowing reed seeds from the air. For many seasons these artificially created reedbeds and marshes provide ideal habitats for wetland birds. However, the ultimate aim of the process is to create farmland, and eventually the reed-beds are replaced.

PEACE AND QUIET

Texel

Without doubt, Texel (the southernmost of the Wadden Islands) is the most outstanding bird-watching location in the Netherlands. The island is also a popular holiday spot and, as such, is an ideal destination for a family, not all of whose members may be keen naturalists.

Texel lies 62 miles (100km) north of Amsterdam and is reached by a regular ferry service from Den Helder (a train service also operates between the capital and the port). Once on the island, bikes can be hired and are an ideal way to explore.

Like the other Friesian Islands, Texel was created by wave action which built up extensive sand dunes. These were gradually colonised and stabilised by marram grass and, over the years, more substantial vegetation developed. Nowadays you can observe the whole succession of habitats as you move away from the North Sea coast – from sand dunes, through dune slacks to marshes and open pools. Grazing meadows and plantation woodland add further dimensions to this already varied island.

Texel is best known for its breeding birds, including such specialities as avocets, marsh harriers, spoonbills and bitterns. Migration times can also be exciting, with large numbers of tired songbirds stopping off on the island to rest and feed.

The island also has considerable botanical and entomological interest. There are numerous protected areas on Texel, including nature reserves, although almost anywhere on the island can be good. Among the best places are the following:

De Geul Nature Reserve, in the south-west of the island, is an area of dunes with scrubland and lagoons. Between 1 March and 30 August the reserve is closed, to protect the breeding birds (conducted tours are available during this period). At other times, visitors can enter the reserve but must keep to the marked paths. Bird-watching highlights include avocets, marsh harriers and spoonbills, while the dune flowers include marsh orchids,

Avocet

This is one of the most distinctive of wading birds. It has bold black and white plumage, long blue legs and a long upturned bill. It is also a fair size, and is not particularly retiring, so you have a good chance of seeing this bird. When feeding, the bill is swept from side to side and small aquatic animals sifted from the water.

Avocets have one of their European strongholds in the Netherlands and Texel is particularly important. They breed here and many spend the winter on the coast. Their nests comprise a 'scrape' close to water, and the shallow dune lakes provide an ideal environment for them.

Grass of Parnassus and round-leafed wintergreen.
De Muy Nature Reserve is an area of dunes dotted with small lakes. Access restrictions apply between 1 March and 30 August as they do at De Geul. The reserve lies on the west coast, just north of De Koog. Spoonbills and marsh and Montagu's harriers are among the highlights.

Nesting spoonbills

Spoonbill

Although superficially resembling a heron or an egret, the spoonbill is easily recognised by its long, spatulate bill. The broad, flattened tip of this remarkable appendage is used to filter out small animals from the water in which the bird searches for food. Spoonbills nest in small colonies, building untidy twig nests in trees and bushes. The colonies on Texel are among the most northerly in Europe. In flight, spoonbills can be identified by their long, trailing legs and extended neck, head and bill.

PEACE AND QUIET

Other Wadden Islands

Terschelling can be reached by ferry from Harlingen. The dune flora here is excellent and there are many interesting breeding birds. There are three nature reserves on the island: the Boschplaat Nature Reserve, which occupies the eastern third of the island, the Terschelling Nature Reserve in the centre, and the Noordvaarder Nature Reserve at the western tip.

Schiermonnikoog can be reached by ferry from Lauwersoog and has excellent dune formations and coastal marshes. **Vlieland** can be reached by ferry from Harlingen and has dunes, heaths, plantations and coastal habitats.

De Wieden Nature Reserve

This large wetland reserve lies in the centre of the country some 75 miles (120km) northeast of Amsterdam. The nearest towns are Meppel and Steenwijk. From Meppel, drive southeast to Baarlo and then turn north and follow roads that cross the reserve until you reach Sint Jansklooster, where there is an information centre. Most of the reserve is inundated and completely inaccessible. However, nature trails allow visitors to explore a small part of De Wieden.

Centuries of peat cutting have helped to make this reserve an outstanding wetland area. Abandoned trenches have lots of exciting marshland flowers, and breeding birds include wildfowl, marsh harriers and bitterns.

De Weeribben Nature Reserve

Lying northeast of De Wieden Nature Reserve, with their borders virtually contiguous, De Weeribben Nature Reserve is another superb wetland area created by peat cutting activities. It lies west of Steenwijk, and there is an information centre and car park at Ossenzijl. A nature trail allows exploration of this otherwise inaccessible area. Spring is a good time to visit both this reserve and the adjacent De Weiden Nature Reserve. Many of the breeding birds will be displaying or singing. Listen for the fluty song of elusive golden orioles among the wetland vegetation. Cetti's warbler has a loud, rasping song, while Savi's warbler delivers an almost mechanical, reeling song which sounds anything but bird-like.

Yellow flag

Practical

This section (with the yellow band) includes food, drink, shopping, accommodation, nightlife, tight budget, special events etc

The native cuisine of the Netherlands is not likely to inspire passion in the gourmet, though you will find good, unpretentious restaurants serving a wide range of fresh fish and seafood. In addition, you will find a rich choice of international cuisines, especially in the larger cities, where you can take your pick of Oriental, Greek, American, Mexican, Italian, Egyptian, Indian and Indonesian food. Indonesian restaurants, in particular, offer very good value for money and are in plentiful supply. They are a reminder of the long-standing Dutch colonial connections with Indonesia. After that country was granted independence in 1949, many Indonesians came to live here and opened restaurants that vary between the truly authentic and those that offer hybrid dishes more suited to Dutch taste. Nearly all Indonesian restaurants serve a choice of *rijsttafel* ('rice table') banquets, with everything from 15–45 separate dishes ranging from mild coconut-based curries to shrimps in fiery hot *sambal* sauce.

Although you will have the most choice in the main cities – Amsterdam above all – most towns and villages offer a choice of eating places. Many restaurants take credit cards and traveller's cheques, but the further into the rural areas of the Netherlands you go, the less likely it is that credit cards will be taken.

'Tourist Menus'
Around 500 restaurants in the Netherlands offer a Tourist Menu at a set price which is fixed each year and is the same wherever you go in the country. Participating restaurants can be identified by their special sign, which consists of a white fork on a blue background, between the words 'Tourist Menu'. These menus are not to be scoffed at; they are usually created specially by the chef and may well feature seasonal specialities. Many restaurants also offer a children's menu (*Kindermenu*), and another 300 or so participate in the *Nederlands Dis* scheme, signifying that they specialise in authentic Dutch or regional specialities – look out for the

FOOD AND DRINK

scheme sign which consists of a red, white and blue soup tureen. Leaflets, annually updated, listing all the restaurants that participate in the schemes, are available from overseas offices of the Netherlands Board of Tourism and from local VVV tourist offices.

Dutch Delicacies

On the whole Dutch food is filling and tends to be high in protein, based around steak, chicken and fish, and with a strong accent on hearty, filling soups and stews. Pea soup (*erwtensoep*) is one traditional dish that you are likely to encounter all over the Netherlands; it is made from dried split peas flavoured with a ham bone or bacon, and is eaten with hunks of bread – it ought to be thick enough to support the weight of a spoon placed upright in the soup. If such rib-sticking dishes do not sound appetising to you, take heart from the fact that the extensive coastline and numerous inland lakes of the Netherlands produce an abundance of good fresh fish. Smoked and salt-cured herrings are very popular and can be bought from street stalls, along with eels, mackerel and other small fish. For a real treat, though, you should find a restaurant specialising in the plump and succulent oysters and mussels of Zeeland. These delicacies are usually to be found all over the Netherlands during the July–April season. Large dishes of vegetables usually accompany the main

dish in a traditional Dutch restaurant and sometimes the quantity is daunting. If you have room at the end of a meal, apple pies and other heavy puddings are the norm.
Also available in plenty are fast-food outlets, serving pizzas, hamburgers, sandwiches and kebabs. A Dutch speciality in the fast-food line is chips; *vlaamse* or 'Flemish' *frites* are the best. Served from vans, stalls and open-air cafés, they are delicious with salt and mayonnaise, stuffed into a cardboard cone and eaten with a little plastic spike.
Pancakes are also a popular cheap option; *pannekoeken* (pancake houses) can be found all over the Netherlands and you can choose between a whole range of sweet and savoury fillings.
The Dutch, like their neighbours the Belgians, are very keen on sweet pastries and cakes. These are often sold from long, half-open wagons in the streets of many towns, and you can smell the hot vanilla and almonds from quite a distance, sweeping through the streets. Waffles are a popular choice, covered in maple syrup. *Poffertjes*, another treat, are the Dutch equivalent to doughnuts; deep-fried dough balls served with lots of butter and a sprinkling of icing sugar. Most stalls have an array of popular cakes, biscuits and pancakes which are filled with cream and jams.
You won't go hungry at a Dutch breakfast table, either: expect to find cereals, fruits and yoghurts as well as a range of

cold meats, cheeses, eggs, toast and croissants, and probably a choice of breads. Dutch coffee is good and strong but tea and hot chocolate are usually on offer too.

Vegetarians are well catered for in the Netherlands and most restaurants feature at least one vegetarian option on their menu.

For an authentic Dutch experience you should make sure to visit at least one **Brown Café**, or *bruin café* – so called because traditionally the walls are brown with age and cigarette smoke. A modern version has sprung up, the designer 'white café', a brighter, more minimalist bar but trying to capture the same atmosphere and informality. Beer is the most popular drink, brewing being a national skill that dates back to medieval times, and there is usually a wide choice available, the local favourites being Heineken,

Oranjeboom, Grolsch and Amstel. All these beers are of the light pilsner type but they can be stronger than they look! Increasingly popular, especially in the cities, is white beer brewed from wheat, with a mild creamy taste, usually served with a slice of lemon for extra bite. Traditional Dutch gin, called *jenever* (juniper) is another popular option. It is usually served ice-cold in a tiny glass in two versions: *jonge* (young) *jenever* is colourless and much like standard gin, but *oude* (old) *jenever* is pale yellow, creamy and aromatic – well worth trying. Brown cafés also serve a wide range of liqueurs made from fruit, and non-alcoholic drinks such as tea and coffee. Any café that styles itself an *eetcafé* will also serve a range of inexpensive dishes such as open sandwiches, various omelettes, and salad.

Freshly smoked fish

SHOPPING

SHOPPING

The specialities of the Netherlands are cheeses, cut flowers, bulbs, pottery and wooden shoes. In addition, Dutch chocolates are almost as well known as their Belgian counterparts and can be bought in most towns. Diamonds and antiques, if you can afford them, are best bought in Amsterdam which is still the centre of the trade. Amsterdam, as a whole, offers the best range of shops in the Netherlands and you can browse for hours among small speciality stores selling everything from Asiatic art to kites, candles and boomerangs. Dutch cheeses can, of course, be bought packaged at any supermarket or food speciality shop, but it is far more fun to buy a whole cheese – especially some of the aged Goudas which are not easily obtainable outside Holland – in one of the cheese towns. Alkmaar, Edam and Gouda all have cheese markets and plenty of possibilities for shopping in their centres. Many cheese specialists here will package your cheese and arrange to have it sent to your home or to a friend you want to surprise with an unusual gift. Flowers and bulbs are available everywhere, but the floating flower-market in Amsterdam (on the Singel canal) is well worth a visit, as are the Keukenhof gardens at Lisse, where you can order bulbs to be sent direct to your home. Seek the advice of florists before you make your

Out for a bargain

purchase – some countries prohibit the import of plant material unless it can be proved that it comes from virus-free stock. Most florists are very knowledgeable about the different import controls and will explain what to do.

Delft in the south and Makkum in the north of the country both make and sell their distinctive hand-painted ceramics. These too are widely available from specialist retailers in the larger cities. Genuine Delft and Makkum pottery is not cheap and should come with an official certificate of authenticity. Cheap imitations are sold in just about every souvenir shop in the Netherlands.

Markets play a major part in the shopping life of the country. All towns have them – usually a general market once or twice a week, plus a specialist market selling bric-a-brac, antiques, books or flowers. Local VVV tourist offices will have details. If you do not want to weigh yourself down with shopping while you are travelling, remember that Schiphol airport has good and extensive shopping facilities. Any visitor from a country outside the European Community is entitled to a refund of the 20 per cent value added tax (BTW) on high-priced purchases (currently refunds are available on goods costing more than f300 in total – not necessarily single items). Any shop displaying the sign 'Holland Tax Free' will explain how to obtain the refund and you can also pick up a leaflet, *Tax Free for Tourists*, at VVV offices.

ACCOMMODATION

There is every kind of accommodation you could wish for in the Netherlands. The general standard is high but there is a direct correlation between price and facilities. There is no shortage of luxury hotels in the main cities and a number of exclusive ones are dotted discretely around the countryside. The hotels are graded according to their facilities rather than their individual charm, and grades range from 5-star to 1-star, priced accordingly (reckon on paying f300 for a double room with bathroom in a 5-star hotel and f85–f100 in a 1-star establishment). You can buy an up-to-date-list of all the hotels in the country, with rates and prices, from overseas offices of the Netherlands Board of Tourism.

As well as hotels there are numerous bed and breakfast places available. Local VVV tourist offices keep a list of private householders in the region who rent out rooms. Prices are excellent and vary according to the season; the price does not usually include breakfast although this will be provided on request and will probably be substantial. Self-catering is another popular option in the Netherlands, particularly by the coast and on the Wadden Islands, and there are many campsites and Youth Hostels spread over the country. Again, lists are available from the Netherlands Board of Tourism and local VVV offices.

Al fresco performance

If you are visiting the Netherlands in the summer (June to August), during the bulb season (April to May) or around Christmas and New Year it would be best to book in advance, especially if you want to stay in Amsterdam. Advance reservation is very easy. You can call the hotel direct – invariably the person who answers the phone will speak English – or you can use the excellent services of the Netherlands Reservation Centre (NRC), PO Box 404, 2260 AK Leidschendam (tel: (070) 320 2500; fax: (070) 320 2611), which are free and cover the whole of the country. If you let them know the dates of your stay and your preferences in terms of price, type of room and hotel, etc., they will handle all the booking for you. Booking forms can also be obtained from offices of the Netherlands Board of Tourism. If you have not made any reservations in advance it is well worth using the VVV tourist offices to help you. They keep extensive lists of all types of accommodation and will make bookings on the spot (but not by telephone) – for rooms anywhere in the Netherlands.

CULTURE, ENTERTAINMENT AND NIGHTLIFE

In the rural areas of the Netherlands you will have to make your own entertainment but the big cities – notably Amsterdam, Rotterdam and Den Haag – offer a feast of options, ranging from top class orchestral, ballet and opera performances to the way-out extremes of the avant garde, plus discos, jazz clubs and live rock music. The VVV tourist office in all three cities publishes a fortnightly English-language listings magazine called *What's On In ...* These publications specifically highlight events that can be enjoyed by non-Dutch speakers. You can also book tickets for most performances at the local VVV office.

WEATHER AND WHEN TO GO

The Netherlands has a maritime climate, which means that winters are rarely very cold and summers are generally mild, with the chance of rain at any time. The east and southeast are slightly colder in the winter and warmer in the summer. Take warm clothes if you are visiting in winter and be prepared for long periods of grey, foggy weather. Take a cardigan and umbrella for the summer so as to be prepared for all eventualities.

In the big cities there is no such thing as a closed season – Amsterdam, for example, is a very popular year-round destination, though you will find it considerably more crowded during the bulb season (April–May) and during the school and university holidays (Christmas, Easter and June to August). In the more rural parts of the Netherlands you will find that the majority of museums and attractions are either closed or have limited opening hours from October to March; on the other hand, this can be the best time to observe wildlife, particularly the large numbers of migrating birds.

SPECIAL EVENTS

Overseas offices of the Netherlands Board of Tourism will supply a comprehensive list of special events throughout the country. The following list covers just a few of the highlights to look out for.

January
Leiden Jazz Festival

February
Pre-Lent carnivals throughout the country, especially in the Catholic provinces of Noord Brabant and Limburg

March
European Fine Art Fair, Maastricht

April
Rotterdam Marathon
Flower parade from Haarlem to Noordwijk

June
Pink Pop, the Netherlands largest country-wide pop music festival

July
International Rose Festival opens in Den Haag, for three months

September
Amsterdam Marathon
State Opening of Parliament, Den Haag

October
International Windsurfing and Beach Motorcycle races, Scheveningen

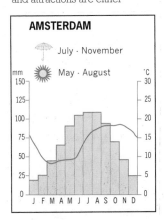

AMSTERDAM

July · November

mm   May · August   °C
150—   — 30
125—   — 25
100—   — 20
75—   — 15
50—   — 10
25—   — 5
0   0
  J F M A M J J A S O N D

HOW TO BE A LOCAL

If you start your travels from Amsterdam you will be immediately struck by the easy-going, friendly and informal nature of the Dutch. Beyond Amsterdam this remains true, but country people are, on the whole, more private and reclusive – always willing to offer help if you need it, but warier of strangers. The Dutch are also renowned for their tolerance and liberal attitudes. Again, there are exceptions to this rule, and in some rural areas a strict form of Calvinism prevails which is at opposite poles to the *laissez faire* attitudes of city dwellers. First-time visitors to major cities may be surprised – even shocked – by the apparent leniency towards drugs, sex and prostitution. There is far more to this than meets the eye, however, and you can spend many a long hour debating the issues with any Dutch people you may happen to meet.

Perhaps the best way of summing up the attitude of most citizens is to say that they believe strongly in the rights of individuals to do as they choose – but they do not approve of the worst exploitative excesses of pornography and drug abuse. Drug abuse, in particular, and its associated crime threatened to get out of hand in the 1980s, resulting in a strong reaction from Dutch citizens who resented the fact that parts of Amsterdam and Rotterdam were becoming 'no-go' areas, unsafe for ordinary people to visit. Groups of local residents have formed themselves into community action groups – with assistance from local authorities – to rejuvenate run-down areas which had been the haunt of pushers and addicts.

This form of community action is typical of Dutch attitudes – they prefer to work by consensus and they resent

Watching the world go by

officialdom and interference. Sadly this means that many Dutch cities are marred by spray-can graffiti and dog faeces, simply because rebellious youths and irresponsible dog-owners alike exploit the tolerance of the majority. On the plus side, the Dutch are proud of their relatively harmonious race-relations record, their policies of equal opportunities for the sexes, and their enlightened attitude to homosexuality – one reason why Amsterdam has numerous clubs for gay men and women.

On a lighter note, the bicycle plays a large part in the lives of many Dutch people both in the city and in the countryside. A popular Dutch pastime, at weekends or holidays, is to set out on a family bicycling expedition, and you will meet many fellow cyclists at picnic and barbecue spots where the atmosphere is relaxed and informal (see also **Cycling Around the Netherlands**, page 113).

Music plays an important part in the lives of many Dutch people, so concerts and music bars offer another opportunity to share genuine local life. An extension of this is the street festival which you will encounter if you are in the Netherlands at carnival time, on the Queen's official birthday (30 April) or at Christmas and New Year. At these times everyone comes out on the streets, celebrating and determined to have a good time – offering a chance to become involved in the local pageantry.

CHILDREN

Children are treated with respect and affection in the Netherlands and the country, as a whole, is very much geared towards the young. All but the grandest restaurants welcome children, and many serve a special *Kindermenu* geared to their tastes. As you travel, look out for swimming pools, special children's museums and *Kinderboerderijen*, children's farms stocked with goats, colourful fowl, guinea pigs and rabbits which young visitors can stroke and feed.

For a visitor it is always difficult to know exactly what is going to suit your children, but here are some definite winners.

Zoos The major zoos in Amsterdam, Amersfoort, Arnhem, Emmen and Rotterdam are excellent places for a day out (opening times and prices from local VVV tourist office).

Museums Many of the hundreds of museums around the country seem purpose-designed to appeal to children. Top of the list are the open-air museums of traditional Dutch life at Arnhem and Enkhuizen, the miniature reconstruction of the Netherlands at Madurodam (Den Haag), the Museon in Den Haag, and the outstanding Nederlands Scheepvaart Museum in Amsterdam. Entrance charges are reduced for children at most museums, and in some places family tickets are available.

Water Fundamental to the Dutch way of life, there is much of the country's struggle with

Cheese choice

the sea that children can understand. The clarity and detail of the Delta Expo exhibition in Zeeland appeals strongly to both children and adults.

Beaches There is no shortage of beaches or resorts in the Netherlands, particularly on the North Sea coast around Den Haag, and on the Wadden Islands.

Bicycles This is an ideal country for children with well-defined, safe cycling tracks which stretch for miles along straight flat lands, and there are always plenty of locals around to ask the way or help if necessary.

Leisure Parks There are a number of these dotted around the country with plenty of entertainment for children. Ask for details at the Netherlands Board of Tourism or at local VVV tourist offices.

Travel Children qualify for reduced rates on public transport throughout the country.

TIGHT BUDGET

The Netherlands is a good choice of destination if you have to travel within a tight budget. There is plenty of cheap accommodation available all over the country. There are many cheap bed and breakfast establishments where you can stay the night and, for a small extra cost, stoke up on an excellent breakfast, which means you will not need to eat again until the evening. These rooms are all bookable through local VVV offices. Cheaper still are the hostels or 'sleep-ins' that provide dormitory accommodation but have decent beds and washing facilities. There are plenty of campsites, and a list and location map can be obtained from the Netherlands Board of Tourism. Cabins are another option: these are basic huts that usually sleep four, known as *trekkershutten*.

Food and Drink There is a huge variety of food and drink available in the Netherlands and a lot of it comes fairly cheap. Inexpensive fast food, snacks, sandwiches (*broodjes*) and *frites* (chips) are available all over the country. If you are staying in the main cities, it is obviously better to explore off the main streets, and you are likely to find less hyped-up prices in small local bars.

Travel A number of travel cards are available which give you cheap travel not only within the Netherlands but also in neighbouring European countries. The *strippenkaart* system can save you money if you buy tickets in bulk (see **Public Transport**, in the **Directory**, page 121), and of course one of the cheapest ways to travel about this country is by bicycle.

CYCLING AROUND THE NETHERLANDS

Cycling is one of the best ways of getting around this country, both in the towns and the countryside. The bicycle is part of the Dutch way of life, and the Netherlands is unique in having a dedicated network of cycle tracks (*fietspaden*) totalling some 6,200 miles (10,000km), complete with their own crossings and traffic lights. In fact you can tour the whole of the Netherlands on these well sign-posted routes, marked by a white bicycle symbol on a blue background.

Bicycles can be hired in almost any town or village. Try the railway station first, if there is one, or enquire at the VVV tourist office. Rates are quoted by the day, half-day or week, and are not expensive, though a deposit is required. Some of the bicycles for hire may seem very old-fashioned; the type favoured by the Dutch is the old, heavy-framed bicycle which has no gears and often no handbrakes (you pedal backwards to stop), so it is sensible to get used to your bicycle before you launch yourself into the traffic.

In the cities, bikes are best parked in bike racks, which you will find all over the place. Never leave your bicycle unlocked.

Cycling is an integral part of the Dutch way of life

Since cycling is so popular, it is rarely difficult to find a bike repair shop in an emergency. The 1:100,000-scale maps (published by the Dutch ANWB motoring organisation and widely available in book shops) show all the cycle paths, and you can obtain a useful information brochure, *Cycling in Holland*, from the Netherlands Board of Tourism; this describes popular routes, with accommodation suggestions. With planning, it is usually possible to avoid the larger towns. At the other end of the scale, some of the long straight roads across the polders can seem interminable. One particular route to be wary of is the road across the top of the Afsluitdijk, the dam across the IJsselmeer; on a windy day, the 19-mile (30-km) journey can be hair-raising, and it is far more relaxing (and safer) to take the ferry between Enkhuizen and Stavoren.

SPORT

The Netherlands offer just about everything a sporty visitor could wish for, including sailing, canoeing, cycling, windsurfing and other water sports. Many campsites offer these, and other options such as horse riding, as standard facilities, so no special arrangements need to be made in advance. You may, however, wish to consult the leaflets and organisations listed below if you have particular requirements.

Canoeing This is a very enjoyable way of seeing some of the most beautiful parts of the country, whistling down canals, dabbling down side streams, or racing across the lakes. For full details of what is available, including hire charges, contact the Netherlands Canoe Association, Postbus 434, 1380 AK Weesp (tel: 02940) 18331).

Fishing This is another popular sport in the Netherlands and the Netherlands Board of Tourism produces a useful publication, *Holland – the Ideal Angling*

Country. This directs you to the right places and gives all the necessary information about rules and regulations.

Golf There are a number of courses open to non-members. Contact the Netherlands Golf Federation, Soestdijkerstraatweg 172, Hilversum (tel: (035) 830565).

Watersports This is the predominant area of sporting activity in the country. It is possible to hire any kind of equipment, including surf-boards and boats of all types and sizes, at any number of watersports centres. You can also hire traditional sailing boats, with crew, for a weekend or longer. Many lakeside marinas offer courses of instruction in sailing and windsurfing. The Dutch motoring organisation, the ANWB, publishes a waterways map, an invaluable companion for those interested in water-based activities. The VVV tourist offices at or near the watersports centres will be able to provide full information for the area.

Regatta time

Directory

This section (with the biscuit-coloured band) contains day-to-day information, including travel, health and documentation.

Contents

Arriving

Entry Formalities You must have a valid passport to enter the Netherlands. A visa is only necessary if you intend to stay for more than three months. Visas should be obtained in advance from Dutch embassies or consulates in your own countries before departure.

By Air Schiphol, the Netherlands main international airport, is located 9 miles (14km) southwest of Amsterdam. Direct flights to Schiphol are available from almost every other international airport in the world. In addition, there are several flights daily from other European airports into Schiphol and the regional airports at Eindhoven, Maastricht and Rotterdam. From the UK, for example, thirteen different airlines offer hourly scheduled services to the Netherlands from London and regional airports, so there is no lack of choice. Commuter flights (around 8.00–10.00hrs and 16.00–18.00hrs) are often booked up well in advance, as are flights at weekends and in summer.

The best way to find bargain flights is to travel mid-week (Tuesday to Thursday) around the middle of the day, and book at least three weeks in advance.

Airport Link Schiphol airport
has its own railway station,
located in the airport complex,
a short walk by escalator from
the arrivals hall. Trains for
Amsterdam Centraal Station
depart every 15 minutes from
06.00–24.00hrs and at hourly
intervals from 01.00–05.00hrs.
The journey into Amsterdam
takes around 20 minutes and
the fare is very cheap. From
Schiphol station you can also
travel south on the line to Den
Haag (The Hague) and
Rotterdam.

By train and ferry There are
good, fast rail connections to
the Netherlands from Belgium
(from Brussels and Antwerp),
from France (Paris) and from
Germany (Köln). From the UK
there is a choice of boat/train
and ferry services as follows:
London (Liverpool Street) to
Amsterdam via Harwich and
the Hook of Holland, boat/train
service, 12 hours, British Rail
European (tel: (071) 834 2345).
London (Victoria) to
Amsterdam via Dover and
Oostend, boat/train service, 10
hours, British Rail European (tel:
(071) 834 2345).
Harwich to the Hook of Holland,
ferry service, 6 3/4 hours by
day, 8 3/4 hours by night,
Sealink/Stena (tel: (0233)
647047).
Hull to Rotterdam, ferry service,
14 hours, North Sea Ferries (tel:
(0482) 77177).
Sheerness to Vlissingen, ferry
service, 7–8 hours, Olau Line
(tel: (0795) 666666).
All these services will take you
direct to the Netherlands but
you should also consider train
and ferry services from the UK

ports of Dover and Ramsgate to
the French ports of Calais and
Dunkerque respectively (or the
hovercraft from Dover to
Calais). There are also services
from Dover to the Belgian port
of Oostende, with the added
possibility of the jetfoil. Details
available from travel agents.
By Bus Hoverspeed City Sprint
(tel: (081) 554 7061) offers a
regular service from London's
Victoria bus station to
Amsterdam via Dover and
Oostend, journey time about 10
hours. Other companies with
services to the Netherlands
from the UK are Eurocity (tel:
(071) 828 8361) and Eurolines
(tel: (0582) 404511).
By Car The Netherlands is
easily reached by car from
northern France, Belgium and
western Germany, and by ferry
service from the UK (see
above). Border formalities are
minimal but you should have
your passport ready just in
case. You will also need to
carry your driving licence (an
International driving licence is
not necessary), the vehicle
registration document,
evidence that the vehicle has
passed a road safety test (MOT
in the UK), proof of insurance
(for example, a Green Card)
and a warning triangle for use
in the event of breakdown (this
is very important as insurance
companies have been known to
refuse to pay out if this was not
displayed). An international
identity disc must be affixed to
the rear of the vehicle.

Camping
The Dutch themselves are keen
campers and you will find

clean, well-equipped campsites all over the Netherlands, although in the case of large cities such as Amsterdam they are usually some way from the city centre. At many sites you can hire bicycles, and sometimes canoes as well. Some sites also have chalets, known as *trekkeshutten* for rent, equipped with beds and cooling equipment. There are some 2,000 sites altogether in the Netherlands and the Dutch motoring organisation, the ANWB, publishes an annual directory with details of facilities and fees and booking forms. This is available in bookshops in the Netherlands or from the ANWB, Wassenaarseweg 220, Den Haag, The Netherlands (tel: (070) 314 7147). Overseas offices of the Netherlands Board of Tourism also supply free leaflets describing selected sites. Within the Netherlands, any branch of the VVV tourist office network will supply you with information on campsites in their locality.

Car Rental

Car rental facilities are available in the arrivals hall at Schiphol airport, and branch offices of the international and local firms are to be found in most main towns. To rent a car you must be over 21 years old, have at least a year's driving experience and be in possession of a valid driving licence.

Crime

Crime is a particular problem in Amsterdam and Rotterdam where professional pickpockets operate and drug addicts, desperate for money, will steal anything they can. Even so, the chances of becoming a victim of crime are no greater than in London or New York, especially if you take a few common-sense precautions.

Do not walk in empty dark alleys or in parks after dark, and avoid red-light districts where the drug pushers operate. Foreign number plates and hired cars act as a magnet for thiefs, so never leave valuables in the car, and do leave your vehicle in a supervised car park whenever possible. As a further precaution women should wear their handbags across their bodies and men keep their wallets in upper pockets, especially while on public transport. Leave valuables and excess cash in your hotel safe.

Customs Regulations

There are no restrictions on the amount of money you can take into or out of the country. Prohibited and restricted goods are: meat, meat products, fruit, plants, flowers, weapons and narcotic drugs. You will find details of the current duty-free

Colourful costumes

DIRECTORY

limits for the import of tobacco, alcohol and toiletries posted in all duty-free shops and at airports, ports and ferry terminals. These are about to be superseded by very generous new allowances which most ordinary travellers will find difficult to exceed.

Disabled Visitors

A free leaflet, *Holland for the Handicapped*, is available from overseas branches of the Netherlands Board of Tourism. This lists hotels, restaurants, museums, galleries and other places of interest which have access and other facilities for the disabled.

As a general rule, the Netherlands has a very active disablement lobby and you will find that the needs of less mobile people are catered for. Even so, hotels located in older buildings often have very steep staircases and no lifts, so it is worth checking their suitability before booking.

Netherlands Railways offer a comprehensive service for the disabled traveller. This includes a free escort service and assistance at all stations, and a timetable in braille. At Schiphol airport there is a desk open daily 06.00–23.00hrs to help disabled travellers through the airport.

Braille is also used to denote the value of Dutch paper currency.

Driving

The Netherlands has an excellent motorway and main road network so that getting from one place to another is quick and easy. Even so, the main roads linking Amsterdam, Rotterdam, Den Haag and Utrecht can be very busy and congested during the morning and evening rush hours (07.30–09.30hrs and 16.30–18.30hrs). You will also find parking in these, and several other cities very difficult. The best course of action is to find a hotel that offers secure parking and forget the car for the duration of your stay in the city. This is especially true of Amsterdam, where vigilant traffic police will clamp your car or tow it away if you break any parking regulations.

Rules of the road Driving is on the right-hand side of the road, and speed limits are 30mph (50kph) in built-up areas, 49mph (80kph) elsewhere and 74mph (120kph) on motorways. Seat belts are compulsory for drivers and front seat passengers.

Fuel Petrol stations are regularly spaced along the main roads and on the edge of towns so you should never be far way from one, and those on national highways are open 24 hours. Unleaded petrol is sold as *Eurosuper* (95 octane, pumps usually green) and *Superplus* (98 octane, pumps usually yellow).

Parking It is best to head straight for a municipal car park when you arrive in a town or city and then explore on foot or public transport. Car parks are usually well signposted – look for a white letter P on a blue background. In most car parks you take a ticket on arrival and pay on exit at a special kiosk or machine before you drive to the exit.

Breakdown Main highways have frequent police patrols and they will help if you are in trouble. Members of a motoring organisation such as the AA can use the 24-hour breakdown services of the Dutch ANWB for free. Look for special roadside telephones or tel: 06-0888. If you do not belong to a motoring organisation recognised by the ANWB you can still use the emergency service, but you will be charged a fee.

Electricity

220 volts. AC plugs have two round pins. Most non-Continental appliances require adaptors and, for North American appliances, a voltage transformer.

Embassies and Consulates

Australia Koninginnegracht 23, 2514 AB Den Haag (tel: (070) 363 0983).
Canada Sophialaan 7, 2514 JP Den Haag (tel: (070) 361 4111).
United Kingdom Lange Voorhout 10, 2514 ED Den Haag (tel: (070) 364 5800).
USA Lange Voorhout 102, 2514 EJ Den Haag (tel: (070) 362 4911)

Emergency Telephone Numbers

National

Police, ambulance and fire: 0611

Amsterdam (code 020)
Police: 6222222
Ambulance: 5555555
Central doctors service (this service includes doctors, dentists and chemists):

6642111
Lost property: 558005

The Hague (code 070)
Police: 3104911
Doctor: 3455300
Dentist: 3974491
Lost property: 3108015

Rotterdam (code 010)
Police: 4242911
Doctor: 4115504
Dentist: 4552155
Lost property: 4242911

Apart from those listed above, most major cities have an emergency doctor and dentist service; details can be found in the front of the local telephone directory – or ask at your hotel.

Calling home

DIRECTORY

Entertainment Information

The larger cities all have their own excellent listings magazines published by the local VVV tourist office which highlight events that can be enjoyed by non-Dutch speakers. These are often distributed free to hotels.Tourist offices will also give you up-to-date information on local events, and handle bookings.

Health

European Community residents can obtain free medical advice and treatment on presentation of an E111 certificate. Forms are obtainable from your doctor or department of health office before you leave home. British visitors can also obtain forms from post offices, contained within the booklet *T2 – Health Advice for Travellers Inside the European Community*. This explains how to get the form validated before you travel, and what to do if you seek medical advice. (Residents of the Irish Republic should apply to their regional health board.) If you are not covered by this scheme it would be wise to take out travel insurance that includes medical cover.

Holidays – Public and Religious

The most important of these are:

New Year's Day
Good Friday
Easter Sunday and Monday
Queen's Birthday (30th April)
Ascension Day
Whit Sunday and Monday
Christmas Day
Boxing Day

Lost Property

See under **Emergency Telephone Numbers**, above.

Media

Newspapers *De Volkskrant* (left of centre), *NRC Handelsblad* (uncommitted) and *De Telegraaf* (right wing) are the three most widely read serious daily newspapers.
Foreign publications, including British and Amercian newspapers and magazines, arrive on the same day they are published and are widely available.
TV and Radio Dutch cable network supply a wide range of TV channels including Britain's BBC1 and BBC2, Sky Channel and Super Channel. English language films are often shown undubbed on Dutch TV channels. The BBC World Service, BBC Radio 4 and Voice of America can all be picked up on radio.

Money Matters

There are no restrictions on the import of foreign currency into the Netherlands. Money can be changed at most banks and post offices, at *bureaux de change*, in hotels and at the VVV tourist office in larger cities. The exchange rates and commissions vary widely, so look around for the best deal, especially when changing large sums. You will often find that the best rate is offered by GWK offices at airports, railway stations and border points. Some of the GWK offices (for example those at Amsterdam Centraal and Schiphol stations) are open 24 hours daily. You can also use GWK offices to change traveller's cheques, and a credit card to obtain cash in advance.

The local currency is the guilder (also called a florin), which is divided into 100 cents. The currency is variously denoted as Dfl, fl, f, HfL or Gld. Credit cards are widely accepted in restaurants, hotels and shops, at stations, and at airline and theatre booking offices.

Museum Card

If you plan to visit a lot of galleries and museums you should invest in a *Museumjaarkaart* (Museum Year Card), which gives you unrestricted admission to more than 350 museums across the country for the calendar year in which it is issued. After about 15 visits to museums the card will have paid for itself. Details are available at all participating museums and at VVV tourist offices. To purchase a Museum Card you will need to supply a passport-sized photograph.

Opening Times

Banks These open Monday to Friday 09.00–16.00 or 17.00hrs, sometimes to 20.00hrs on late-night shopping evenings (usually a Thursday or Friday). **Shops** are usually open Monday to Friday 08.30 or 09.00 to 17.30 or 18.00hrs, Saturday to 17.00hrs. Shops close on Sunday, although you may find some grocery or tourist shops open in the big cities. Many shops and department stores also close on Monday mornings, and all shops must close for one half-day a week by law. Every shop

displays details of its opening hours on the door or window. In some rural towns shops also shut for the lunch hour. Shops open late (until 21.00) one day a week in big cities, usually on a Thursday or Friday.

Museums/Galleries These are usually open from Tuesday to Saturday 10.00–17.00hrs, and Sundays 13.00–17.00hrs. Many are closed on Monday, and those outside major cities may well be closed during October to March.

Pharmacies

Drug stores (*Drogisterij*) sell non-prescription medicines, such as aspirin. For prescription drugs you need an *Apotheek*, staffed by trained pharmacists, who are also happy to treat minor ailments. They are usually open Monday to Friday 08.00 or 09.00–17.30 or 18.00hrs. VVV tourist offices and hotels will know which are open in the evenings and at weekends.

Places of Worship

Most faiths have services in the larger cities. Ask at VVV tourist offices.

Police

See under **Emergency Telephone Numbers** above.

Post Office

You will find a post office (PTT) in every town, usually open Monday to Friday 08.30–17.00hrs, Saturday 08.30–12.00hrs. Larger offices in the cities have an outer hall which stays open later, with stamp machines and telephones. Post boxes have two slots, one for local mail and one for abroad. Stamps can also be bought from many souvenir shops and tobacconists. It costs less to send a postcard than a letter.

Public Transport

Air NLM City Hopper (tel: (020) 6170931) operates services from Amsterdam to Eindhoven and Maastricht, and between Groningen and Enschede.

Bus Long distance bus and train travel is co-ordinated throughout the Netherlands and provides access to all towns and villages. A guide produced by Netherlands Railways, called the *Nationale Buswijer*, is invaluable for the traveller as it lists bus routes, times, zones, prices and includes useful maps.

Bicycles See under **Cycling Around the Netherlands**, page 113.

Canal Boats In most cities and towns where canals are a feature there is likely to be a canal boat service. It is often an excellent way of getting your bearings in a city, especially in Amsterdam. VVV tourist offices will have details of the services available.

Coach Tours Numerous operators offer inexpensive coach tours covering the most popular places of interest, especially in the region of Amsterdam. Your hotel and the local VVV tourist office will have details of what is available.

Metro, City Bus and Tram The Netherlands has an excellent integrated public transport system, which means in effect that the same tickets can be used anywhere in the country on trams and buses and – in the case of Amsterdam and Rotterdam – on the metro and local railways as well. Two types of ticket are available: Rover Cards (*Dag Kaarten*) are valid for one or more days (up to nine) unlimited travel. Alternatively you can buy strips of tickets, *Nationale Strippenkaart,* which can be used for individual journeys. *Strippenkaart* are sold in strips of 6, 10, 15 and 45 tickets, and the more you buy the bigger the discount. Both types of ticket can be bought at VVV tourist offices, railway stations and at many tobacconists and newsagents (they are also available from the driver, but this is more expensive). All transport routes in the Netherlands are divided into zones; every journey automatically costs one ticket and then one extra ticket for each zone you travel through, i.e. two tickets are cancelled for one zone, three tickets for two zones, etc. You fold the *strippenkaart* to feed the required number of tickets into the stamping machines at the entrance to the bus or tram, or at the metro station barriers. The tickets are then valid for one hour of travel and you can change from one route to another or from one form of transport to another without using any more strips, provided you remain within the same zones.

Trains All the main cities of the Netherlands are linked by a network of cheap and efficient express trains. From

Amsterdam, for example, virtually the whole of the Netherlands is accessible by means of a train journey of 2 hours at most, and often 1 hour or less. Trains depart along the main intercity routes at hourly or half-hourly intervals. Enquire at station offices for details of special deals.

Rover tickets will save you a lot of money if you are going to make extensive use of railways, and there are many excursion packages to popular destinations which include discounts on the transport cost and admission fees (ask for *NS Dagtochten*).

Senior Citizens

Some museums offer reduced price admission to senior citizens but often concessions are only available to Dutch citizens.

Student and Youth Travel

Young people and students can buy discounted rover tickets for use on the railways and on public transport. There are nearly 50 official youth hostels in the Netherlands, supplying dormitory accommodation and cheap meals to those with an international youth hostel card. Cheap student accommodation is on offer in some university towns during the summer. Contact VVV tourist offices for details.

Telephones

Public telephones in the Netherlands are automatic and allow you to dial direct. Coin-operated phones take 25c, f1 and f2.50 pieces, or you can buy a phonecard – sold at

Bargain-price accommodation

newsagents and tobacconists in 20, 40 or 100 units – and use a card-operated phone (*kaarttelephoon*). Card-operated phones are being introduced in larger cities that will allow you to use your credit card instead. Calls can also be made from post offices and from 'Telehouse' booths, where you make your call and settle up afterwards.

To call overseas, dial the international code 09; when the tone changes dial the country code (Australia 61, Eire 353, New Zealand 64, UK 44, USA and Canada 1); finally dial the area code, minus the initial 0, and the subscriber number.

Time

The Netherlands observes Central European Time, which is one hour ahead of Greenwich Mean Time during the winter. Clocks here go forward one hour towards the end of March and back again near the end of September. You should note that all air and ferry departures are quoted in local time, as are the arrival times.

Tipping

A service charge is almost always included in a hotel and restaurant bill; adding anything extra is optional but not expected. Taxi meters include a service charge, although it is customary to round up fares to the nearest guilder.

Toilets

These are always easier for men to find than women, since a number of Dutch towns have old-fashioned street-urinals. There are not many public toilets, though you will usually find adequate and clean facilities in museums and department stores, and at motorway service stations. Cafés provide toilets for the use of customers, so you may have to pay the price of a cup of tea or coffee to use them.

Tourist Offices

For leaflets and brochures on the country as a whole, plus specific areas (what to see, accommodation, services and other facilities) contact the **Netherlands Board of Tourism (NBT)** in your own country:
Australia 6th Floor, 5 Elizabeth Street, Sydney NSW 2000 (tel: (02) 247 6921).
Canada 25 Adelaide Street East, Suite 710, Toronto, Ontario M5C 1Y2 (tel: (416) 363 1577).
UK 25–28 Buckingham Gate London SW1E 6LD (tel: (071) 630 0451).
USA 355 Lexington Avenue (21st floor), New York NY 10017
(tel: (212) 370 7367)

(also offices in Chicago and San Francisco)
A charge is made for much of the literature on offer. The NBT can also supply a list of VVV tourist offices in the Netherlands.
VVV offices are generally open Monday to Friday 09.00–17.00hrs, Saturday 10.00-12.00hrs; also evenings and Sunday afternoons during the summer. Offices in the main towns and cities are generally open longer hours.

LANGUAGE

The Dutch will consider it a compliment if you try and speak their language. They may smile at your attempts at pronunciation but don't be put off. It is not easy to reproduce the glottal, gutteral sounds that make up the Dutch language, but practice makes perfect. Even if you do not speak Dutch, language is rarely a problem. Signs and restaurant menus are produced in English as well as Dutch, and a very high proportion of Dutch people speak English fluently – almost everyone in the cities, and most people born since 1945 in the rural areas. Their fluency can make the visitor lazy but the following words and phrases are useful;

yes ja

no nee

please alstublieft

thank you dank u or dank u wel

hello dag

good morning/afternoon/ evening goede morgen/middag/avond

are you well? hoe gaat het met u?

very well uitstekend

excuse me pardon

I come from England Ik kom uit England

breakfast ontbijt

dinner diner

sandwich broodje

cup of coffee/tea kopje koffie/thee

dish of the day daschotel

may I order? mag ik even bestellen?

Stopping for a chat

how much does this cost? wat kost dit?

inclusive of VAT and service charge inclusief BTW en bedieningsgeld

open open

closed gesloten

no entry verboden toegang

a ticket to ... een kaartje naar ...

one way ticket enkele reis

return retour

where's the ...? waar is het ...?

post office postkantoor

chemist apotheek

hospital ziekenhuis

doctor dokter

station station

bank bank

postcard briefkaart

letter box brievenbus

telephone booth telefooncel

diversion omleiding

all directions alle richtingen

through traffic doorgaand verkeer

danger gevaar

no overtaking inhaalverbod

one een

two twee

three drie

four vier

five vijf

six zes

seven zeven

eight acht

nine negen

ten tien

To try to speak Dutch you will need a dictionary and a pronunciation guide. There are a few basic rules that may help with pronunciation: *ee* is pronounced 'ay'; *g* on its own is a guttural sound almost like an h; *j* is normally soft as in 'yah' for *ja* (yes); *oo* is usually shorter than it appears, to make the sound 'oh'; *ij* is pronounced 'eye'. Dutch has similar roots to Flemish and German, so you will find that most Dutch people have some knowledge of both languages, as well as French.

Acknowledgements

The Automobile Association wishes to thank to thank the following photographers and libraries for their assistance in the preparation of this book.

All photos by EDDY POSTHUMA DE BOER except:
J ALLAN CASH PHOTOLIBRARY 54 Bridge, 79 Potato crop;
AMSTERDAM HISTORICH MUSEUM 12 Painting; INTERNATIONAL PHOTOBANK 5 Windmill; Kinderdijk; MARY EVANS PICTURE LIBRARY 10 William the Silent, 11 Calvinists of Antwerp; NATURE PHOTOGRAPHERS LTD 97 Swallowtail (Kevin Carlson), 99 Grey heron (Paul Sterry), 101 Spoonbill (Kevin Carlson), 102 Yellow flag (Paul Sterry); NETHERLANDS BOARD OF TOURISM 6 Kurhaus, 31 Market, 32 Enkhuizen, 34 Keukenhof, 45 Scheveningen, Brown café, 70 Bloemenmarket, 74 Paleis Het Loo; SPECTRUM COLOUR LIBRARY 27 Nightclubs, 76 Grote Kerk; WYN VOYSEY 29 Waterlooplein, 108 Dam, 110 Leidesplein, 112 Market, 119 Phone box, 123 YH sign; WORLD PICTURES cover, Kinderdijk; ZEFA PICTURE LIBRARY (UK) LTD 7 Texel, 18 Keixersgracht, 20 Canal tour; 125 Windmill

INDEX